ASCENT

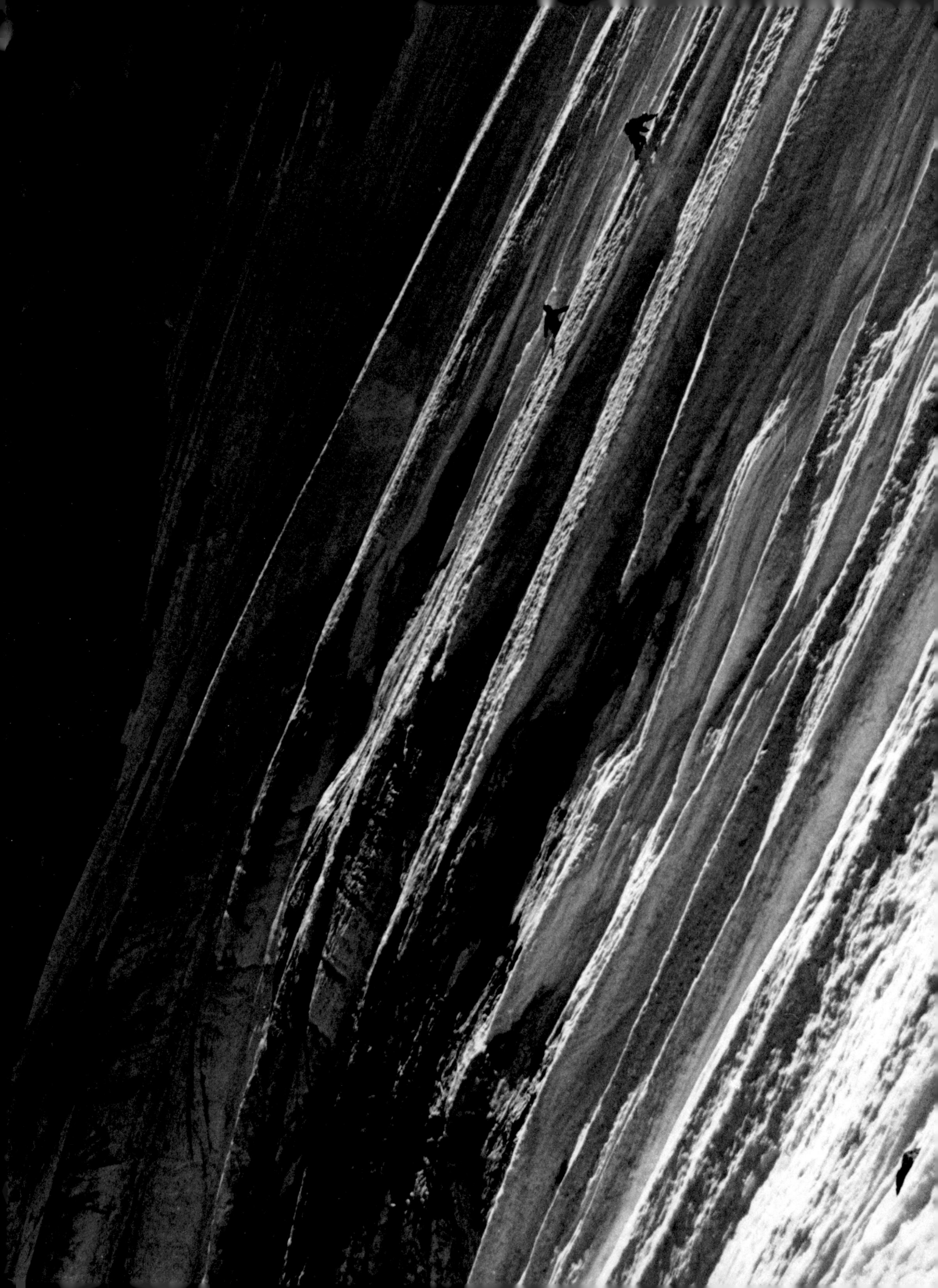

ASCENT
1975 · 1976

THE
MOUNTAINEERING
EXPERIENCE
IN
WORD
AND
IMAGE

SIERRA CLUB BOOKS · SAN FRANCISCO

The Sierra Club, founded in 1892 by John Muir, has devoted itself to the study and protection of the nation's scenic and ecological resources—mountains, wetlands, woodlands, wild shores, and rivers. All Club publications are part of the nonprofit effort the Club carries on as a public trust. There are some 50 chapters coast to coast, in Canada, Hawaii, and Alaska. Participation is invited in the Club's program to enjoy and preserve wilderness everywhere. Address: 530 Bush Street, San Francisco, California 94108.

Matters relating to sales and distribution of Ascent should be sent to Sierra Club Books at the above address. All editorial material must be sent to Ascent, 1398 Solano Avenue, Albany, California 94706.

Copyright © 1976 by Sierra Club Books
All rights reserved
ISBN: 87156-189-1
Manufactured in the United States of America

Credits

Front cover: On the first ascent of the north face of the North Twin, Canada; photo by George Lowe. Frontispiece: In the Bergell Alps; photo by John Cleare. Copyright page: Photo by Gordon Wiltsie. Page 22: Fairview Dome: Photo by Tom Higgins. Pages 24 & 25: Photos by Jim Stuart. Page 26: The Devil's Thumb; photo by U.S.F.S. Pages 58 & 62: Illustrations by A. D. McCormick from Conway's *The Alps from End to End*. Pages 66, 68, & 69: Illustrations are from Charles Nordhoff's 1873 edition of *California for Travellers and Settlers*. Page 76: Photo by Dan Burgette. The article *Lo que el alpinista* was obtained in a mysterious fashion; the Spanish conception of climbing dates back at least to the 1930s. Pages 110 & 113: Photos by John Cleare. Page 114: Photo by Steve Roper. Page 117: The north side of Temple Crag, Sierra Nevada; photo by Jan Tiura. Page 119: Photo by Dick Isherwood. Page 121 (top): From the 1867 edition of *Johnson's Family Atlas*. Page 123: Photo by Roger Breedlove. Page 124: Glacier detail, Alaska; photo by Jim Stuart. Page 125: Photo by Steve Roper. Page 126: Spires and volcanos on the Alaska Peninsula; photo by Jim Stuart. Page 127: Illustration by Allison Clough. Page 128: Photo by Gordon Wiltsie. Back cover: Unnamed and unclimbed peak near Chogolisa, Karakoram Range, Pakistan; photo by Galen Rowell.

PREFACE

What sets Ascent *apart from all similar publications is its whimsicality. While serious about climbing, there is nevertheless always the background chuckle —the healthy midsummer Night's absurdity of it all. It is a delightful and tasteful melange of mountaineering; an eclectic potpourri of adventure, polemics, cartoons, photographs, poetry, humor, and information, all strung together with a few central threads: California climbing, significant mountaineering successes, and* belles-lettres *of alpinism.*

Royal Robbins, one of the most talented and revered climbers I know, wrote these lines on the occasion of the first *Ascent* in 1967. With this appearance of our ninth publication, the first in book format, I feel confident that Robbins' comments are still valid; indeed, we have expanded our treatment of mountain literature to cover all parts of the world, from Turkey to New Guinea.

Editors have come and gone from the masthead since the early days, climbing friends all of them: Joe Fitschen, Dave Dornan, Dave Roberts, Chuck Pratt, Edgar Boyles, and Glen Denny are no longer with *Ascent*, but their editorial and graphic influence can be seen in the early issues. The 1967 *Ascent* cost $1; as we learned later, this was a bit underpriced. As inflation caught hold, and printing costs soared, the price of subsequent issues naturally increased. The 1975 issue was to be priced at $7. Then, in June of that year, I began to think in terms of a book format, something that could accomplish two things: permit a more professional nationwide distribution as part of the Sierra Club's book program, and, more important, provide the editors with more pages to explore a new medium which could better portray the literature and photography of mountaineering. The Sierra Club's publication group encouraged us on the project, and so now we have our book and can only leave it to our readers to tell us if we have done a proper job.

I regret that there is so little space in which to acknowledge our contributors. Some are authors in their own right: Chris Jones (*Climbing in North America*), Galen Rowell (*The Vertical World of Yosemite* and a forthcoming Sierra Club book on the Karakoram), and Harvey Manning (many titles on the North Cascades and also chairman of the editorial committee which produced *Mountaineering: The Freedom of the Hills*). Jeffery Long, Tom Higgins, and Fred Beckey have already appeared in previous issues of *Ascent*. The remainder of our contributors are new this year: Kenneth Andrasko and Dennis Schmitt write about the remote Brooks Range of Alaska; Geoffrey Childs gives us a satirical Himalayan journal; Dan Burgette and Larry Hamilton relate accounts of epic climbs; Eric Sanford portrays Yosemite's modern climbing scene; and Chris Kopczynski and Chic Scott write of the notorious Eiger (the former was a member of the first American ascent, and the latter was part of the film team for *The Eiger Sanction*). Artists Carol Ingram and Allison Clough deserve special mention for their imaginative drawings, and we look forward to further contributions from them. Also, we hope to hear again from photographers Jack Turner, Gordon Wiltsie, Bob Godfrey, and Dudley Chelton, whose fine photographs appear in this volume. Our thanks to you all.

Speaking of the future, I do know that we will be publishing again in the spring of 1978; we already have some material in mind, and certain writers have indicated a desire to contribute essays, articles, and photographs. But there are still many empty pages. We are always looking for writers, photographers, poets, illustrators, and cartoonists with specific comments on the mountaineering scene. If you care, write us about your ideas, request a copy of our contributors sheet, or let us review your manuscript or photographs. We shall be reviewing material for the next volume in early 1977. Send manuscripts and photographs to *Ascent*, 1398 Solano, Albany, CA 94706.

Finally, I would like to express my admiration for my editorial colleagues, Lito Tejada-Flores, Jim Stuart, and Steve Roper, whose talents surpass my own—and to say simply that it has been a great source of enjoyment over these past nine years to have been the catalyst responsible for bringing these diverse personalities together in the production of this publication.

Allen Steck
Berkeley, Calif.
May 18, 1976

EDITORS

ALLEN STECK
LITO TEJADA—FLORES
JIM STUART
STEVE ROPER

CONTENTS

NORTH TWIN, NORTH FACE	chris jones	8
DREAM ASCENTS	carol ingram	16
IN THANKS	tom higgins	22
SOUTHEAST ALASKA	fred beckey	26
POONTANGA	geoffrey childs	38
SONGS OF THE VERTICAL DESERT	gordon wiltsie	44
LEADERSHIP	harvey manning	50
MOUNT DICKEY	galen rowell	52

RESURRECTION	jeffery long	58
SPRING WEEKEND LOVE AFFAIR	eric sanford	66
BALTORO	jack turner	70
SMILEY'S INITIATION	dan burgette	76
LO QUE EL ALPINISTA	anonymous	78
JANUS	bob godfrey & dudley chelton	82
THE AEOLIAN WALL	larry hamilton	88
BROOKS RANGE	kenneth andrasko & dennis schmitt	92
THE EIGER	chris kopczynski & chic scott	98
BOOKS	a collection of reviews	110

NORTH TWIN NORTH FACE
CHRIS JONES

YESTERDAY all was indecision. The north faces above the Columbia Icefields were plastered in ice. Could North Twin be any different? We had gambled on the beginning of August for our attempt, had traded our fear of a rival team for our knowledge of ice conditions. All July we anxiously awaited news from Canada. But now, when all seemed ready, we faltered. Should we give it a few days to clear? Should we go to Robson and come back later? Fear was countered by desire, caution by competition. No matter what alternatives we dreamed up, we could not avoid the basic issue. Were we ready for North Twin, or were we kidding ourselves? We packed our gear.

One foot up, pause, and then the other. It was much like any other uphill grind with a heavy pack. Yet there was a difference. In a few moments we would be at Woolley Shoulder, and I would have my first view of the fabled north face of North Twin. I became strangely detached. I saw George Lowe and myself as figures in the past. I saw our attempt as something that happened long ago. There was a clear sense that it had some meaning for a future generation, but what it was I could not say. More importantly, I knew this would be a very personal moment. I was intrigued to know my limits, wanted to push myself as never before. I had a feeling that North Twin might provide the answer. When I reached the Shoulder I ducked into the wind and glanced across at our face. I was impressed. . . .

All photos by author and George Lowe

THERE WAS NO alternative. I chipped away at the ice in the back of the crack, bridged up the groove, and repeated the performance. It was our fifth day on the wall. We had hoped to be up in three days, but the scale and the difficulties were unrelenting. We had equipment for a typical mixed climb, but the two-thousand-foot upper wall was of Dolomitic steepness and severity. One of our Bluet cartridges had been damaged in the haul bag, and without gas there would be no water to drink. The intricate routefinding had necessitated retreats and pendulums, and together with the gear we had simply dropped or failed to remove, we were down to a dozen pitons and nuts.

George put in a lead and called for me to come up. When I arrived he pointed to a ramp that led around a corner. Was this the connection to the ice gully that led through the headwall? Excited and relieved I led upwards; the ramp gave out on a blank wall. I then tried to reach the headwall above me. The rock was poor and I could not get any satisfactory anchors. Thoroughly despondent, I asked George to take over the lead. He worked hard and unearthed a couple of nut placements, then started up the headwall. A knifeblade, a sky-hook, a thin blade. Slowly he inched up. Now he needed a regular angle. The only one was the principal belay anchor; so I tied off the ropes, stood in a sling, and hammered at it. Suddenly the rope jerked upward. "God, he's off," I thought as I grabbed for the belay rope. In a flash I saw the last piton pull, saw the tremendous wrench on the remaining belay anchor. Then all was quiet. George bobbed up and down at the end of his rope.

I was tense. I insisted we have a rest, eat lunch, and talk over the situation. Four thousand feet up this wall was no place to start taking leader falls. But George was pissed. He wanted to get back on the rock right away. Not up the same crack, he was sure of that, but up a nearby depression. As he started up an even less promising line, it began to snow. He doggedly tried this line, but it was hopeless; another was equally bad. Finally he traversed leftward around the base of the headwall. After an age he returned through the falling snow. It was almost dark, but he had seen the ice gully which led through the headwall. It was a hundred feet away from his high point and was vertical water ice. Maybe we could pendulum into it, then tie the ropes together and protect the lead by leapfrogging our three ice pitons. Even George could not hide the fact that this was a desperate proposal.

The bivouac was austere. We perched on ice-crusted rocks with our feet thrust into our climbing sacks. After a cup of soup and a mouthful of cheese we settled into the bivouac sack. My mind raced. We were in a hell of a spot. We had almost no climbing gear. With our limited means the headwall appeared impossible. The ice gully seemed like madness. Retreat was out of the question; that option had been closed since the day before. The storm was now serious. Snow covered the rock. Tomorrow we would be overdue, and warden Hans Fuhrer would be concerned. But even if he flew in to look for us, what could he do to help? Did we really imagine that they could pull us off this wall? Besides, how long could we hold out?

George was also awake. He must have been going through the same gyrations. Finally we began to talk. He had come to the same conclusion — the only way out was up. We both had been badly rattled, I when the hoped-for exit ramp turned to nothing, and George, when he unthinkingly attacked the headwall after his fall. We were near our limit. Well, if this were the real thing, I was damn glad I was with George. He was solid. I told him of my confidence, and he replied that he felt the same way. I might be lousy on 5.10, but he reckoned I had a high survival potential. As we discussed the options, confidence returned. Conversation died out and we fell asleep.

Chris

IT WAS the seventh day. I headed into the bleak nothingness of a white-out on the Columbia Icefields. Behind me, George kept us on a compass bearing. Yesterday we had lucked out. During a lull in the storm we had made an improbable lead into the ice gully. Fifteen leads of ice climbing in continual storm had brought us to the summit ridge at dusk. Now all we had to do was find the col that gave access to the valley. At mid-afternoon we headed down a dip in the glacier. Just then we heard an unmistakable sound: a helicopter was circling in the valley below. They were looking for us! The noise grew faint and then went away. We crossed a shoulder and plunged into a snow basin; at last we could see where we were going.

Suddenly the noise returned; the helicopter shot over the col. We rushed headlong down the slope, oblivious to the crevasses. The pilot spotted us and swung the machine over in our direction. "You guys ok?" came over the loud-hailer. Apparently satisfied by our shouts and waves, the helicopter circled away. As abruptly as they had arrived they were gone.

The emotional impact was devastating. We realized that someone cared about us, that we were not alone. The last few days had been overwhelming. We had crossed the undefineable line. Now the tensions were released. As I walked toward the valley, tears ran down my face. □

DREAM ASCENTS
CAROL INGRAM

IN THANKS
TOM HIGGINS

Hey Kamps,

The herds of climbers in Tuolumne have dynamited whatever selfish hope I had for sanctuary in the Meadows. Man, you can't even steal a shower at the Tuolumne Lodge without hearing from the adjoining stall an announcement of the newest line. Bunches of Valley climbers and a frenzy of L.A. youth have shot through the place . . . remember seeing them in the Meadows store with hardware on? Vern Clevenger's looseleaf bundle of routes looks like an underground journal, a cauliflower ballooning in the rough. God. As many new routes in two years as in the previous twenty!

Now and then I deride myself for my blatant self-interest. But then I wonder how any climbers—never mind me—can ever again hope to find that rush of loneliness amid the quiet space of high Tuolumne rock.

For all my complaining, only one young lion has homed in on the greatest wall in Tuolumne, the west face of Fairview. Clevenger did the left-facing arch system—remember?—on the right margin of the west face. Get the name—"Mr. Toad's Wild Ride."

Now, he and I are going to try to complete the west face route you and I started in 1968, the direct line in the center of the face. We've been to the high point where you and I retreated, though by three more clean and direct pitches than those you and I originally did. Since then, impatient soul that he is, Clevenger recruited Bob Harrington and together they climbed the sixty-foot smooth headwall above our 1968 highpoint. They took all day, trading leads on ten-foot sections to get the bolts in.

Neither Vern nor Bob made all the moves, and at one point a bolt served as aid to get another in. So, we'll see if it all goes free.

If we get the entire route, it will be the finest on Fairview, if not in Tuolumne; better than Mr. Toad's says Clevenger, and better than the other nearby giant, Fairest of All, which hooks too wildly right in the middle to be the grandest west face line.

This will be my finale in the Meadows . . . last hurrah . . . pièce de résistance. There just don't seem to be more good lines between lines between lines between lines in Tuolumne. Pratt steals away some summers to a secret rock palace which leaves his eyes sparkling most of the fall . . . got to pry it out of him somehow.

Bob, the years I've spent climbing in Tuolumne were pure nourishment to me. How about you? The Meadows always made the regular, flat world bearable, and the flat world made the meadows a sanctuary. It was the pull between the two which nourished. School and work without the mountains would have been deadly. The mountains without the nervous struggling down below would have been limbo, not heaven.

Well, man, as if you didn't know, you were like a father to me for those summers, modeling a conniving, effortless style, clever protection, and witty love for those soaring virgin walls. So, I'll say thanks and thanks also to Tuolumne for holding us like a mother might between deep blue and granite folds in the warmth of the Meadows sun . . . .

Tom

Bob Harrington is kind enough to carry an enormous sack of gear to the base of the wall at seven in the morning. We will begin perhaps 100 yards uphill from Fairest of All. I ask him if he's sure he doesn't want to come along, thinking of the work he put into the route thus far. No, he says, simply and without a trace of envy, he must be in the Valley later in the day. Clevenger takes off at the first lead; it is his third time over the pitch and my second. There is one short section of 5.9. Then we begin the haul. In the sack are an embarrassing assortment of goods, including two sleeping bags, two hammocks, probably thirty bolts, ten drills, food, water, chalk, and no less than three pairs of shoes in addition to those already on our feet! High on the proposed line is an enormous, leaning arch which promises difficult crack climbing; so we carry crack shoes as well as the face-climbing shoes we are wearing.

Even this ballast tank of brazen aids fails to quell all our fears. Vern claims his bowels are bubbling. Mine are jumbled too, probably because I didn't sleep most of the night, too fearful and excited about the sweep of this wall.

The next pitch is sweet and simple, straight up over the golden glaze of undulations so characteristic of Tuolumne rock. Above, blue begins to steep the gray morning sky. Again we haul Santa's sack. As Vern leads the next pitch, again 5.9, I hang, butt out, in the belay seat, looking down on the 70-degree rock, goosebumps flaring up over my head and neck. Ten fewer knobs and we might not even be here!

Soon we join the beginning of the last pitch Kamps and I had managed to climb in 1968. He and I had arrived at this point from several erratically weaving pitches over poorer rock, coming up far to the right of our present line. Vern leads it, remarking again how solid is the 5.10. In following, I smirk to myself at the thought that we were climbing such things eight years ago.

We stand on a dike at the end of the pitch and look around. I recall that the dike runs intermittently left all the way to the regular route, several hundred yards away. A girdle traverse crosses my mind!

Looking up, I see Clevenger and Harrington have created the most remarkable pitch to date in all of Tuolumne. There are no cracks or knobs for forty feet, only scattered, sharp edges the width of pencil lead, with perhaps a few the width of a pencil itself. Most of the seven bolts protecting the sixty-foot pitch clearly were placed in the middle of 5.8 or 5.9 moves.

I am reminded of the many Tuolumne first ascents Kamps and I did where we stood below an improbable section nervously talking until we pushed the climbing into the realm of possibility. How alone, if not adolescent, we seemed then, thrilled and jangled by the thought of no one to see or help us, only the domes standing witness, their polish gleaming like the eyes of cold and riveted fathers. We moved gingerly under the stare, and the Meadows gave us, together or with others, glorious routes: Chartres, Vision, Sweet Jesus, Lucky Streaks, Fairest of All, and more. Why, I wonder, were there just enough holds to allow us to climb, as if the rock were fashioned by benevolent beings?

Suddenly, I feel Vern and I should stop. I feel the rock has given enough, that we are rich enough, that I have grown up enough with the help of this place, that we should thank the wall, give it a pat and rappel. How much can we be expected to find, enjoy, or learn? As I look down, I imagine a balance swinging, our lives in one pan and in the other an ever-increasing stack of weights, each equaling another moment of risk taking. And when our moments are enough to bring down the pan . . . ? I nearly say all this to Vern, as he fiddles with his anchor, getting set for the possibility of an avalanche of falls. Only then do I realize I am bewitched. The pitch has not been climbed in its entirety, nor has the wall above been climbed. We are yet young. There is more here for the taking. The maiden is befuddling me! With that thought, a familiar lust wells up, and in the next moment I feel something like rage.

I clamp over holds past the first bolt to the second. The move by the second is a high step up on pencil lead to a pencil. It's 5.10. The next move, where aid was used to place the next bolt, is all on pencil lead. It's solid 5.10. The next, the next, the next . . . all are 5.10. Is this 5.11?

Midway through the pitch, it begins to seem dumb. The rage ebbs. Each contortion hurts and staggers me. Then I find a knob and begin hopping from one foot to another, thinking this will rest my calves. The motion reminds me of a badly burned insect, fluttering and flopping before death.

Soon, there is a brain whisper, all jumbled like bearings scattered off a shop table. "Do. Go. Wrong foot, but do. Why have I . . . ?" The whispering is me but not me. It is like a possession. "Just do. Fall up. Something. Try that. Do. Do." Outside myself, I watch a foot near my shoulder. I'm catapulting over little sections, prying and foaming, a little crying sound bubbling out. "Lovely horrible. Lovely horrible." It's a veritable ricochet of thought bits, not passion, not tactic, but a precious drop of madness. "It goes. Lovely horrible goes. Bitch! Sweet bitch! Foot flake. Nail hold. Enough. Go! There! Go!" Finally, there is a platform for most of my foot. With rest, the fire fades and logic returns. The last move to a belay ledge, again 5.10, becomes mere geometry compared to the exorcism below. I pinch the underside of a rock nostril, stem left to a downsloping, button-sized hold, ease onto it and cascade onto the belay ledge.

Vern follows with beautiful care and control, but, at one place, suddenly and sharply falls and snaps flat against the rock, proof positive it is a pitch for schizophrenics. Back on the rock, Vern machines through the sequence of moves, his hair a great giggle. We sit down and laugh like cowboys. There is no pitch like this as far as the eye can see. It is a threshold between the standards of 1968 and those of 1974, a gate between exacting skill and a touch of madness. I tell Vern that he and Harrington have devised a masterful pitch, but God save us from another like it above! We speculate that if benevolent beings created the pitch, they knew nothing entrances us like torture.

As Vern zooms off to link up with a long, handsome, right-curving arch, I imagine Poppa Kamps climbing along with us, feet splayed out sideways, edging in his distinctive, duck-like style. Bob's climbing has always been sane, I think, utterly sane. How would he do here? The pitch is sanely protected, but madly difficult. My mind wanders to Frank Sacherer, who reportedly and supposedly thrived on unprotected leads. I think of him throwing himself at a pitch in Yosemite, risking all, I suppose, in hopes of finding all. What a contrast to Kamps, tediously protecting every difficulty, risking little, not aiming for the big bang. How fitting that Bob caught Sacherer's eighty-foot plunge on Lower Rock in Yosemite, held and single-handedly rescued him, unconscious for half the descent. And that Sacherer has, apparently, all but left rockclimbing while Bob, in his mid-forties, climbs on.

But if Bob is sane, he is also wry, too damn wry for me to have ever been able to thank for my introduction to climbing and this place. So, I turn to the imaginary figure climbing the pitch with us, wait until he's exhausted and say, "Hey, thanks."

Vern calls on belay from his perch. He juts out from the leaning arch like a gargoyle. Following, I find the lieback an arching 5.9. My pitch involves a skittering, rock-slapping, 5.10 flaring jam. Vern's lead—ending the arch—is again 5.10, this time an awful undercling over slightly decomposed rock. The rock crinkles under his feet as he jigs across. A hilarious flopping around on my part gets us over the arch at its thinnest portion. Again, there are just enough knobs. From here, one traversing pitch to the left and three more straight up, none over 5.8, gain the top. Over each pitch, we exhaustedly yank the dead walrus along, its nose diving under roofs, its fat flanks melting around every knob in its path. How fitting, I think, that we should be obliged to drag our armory, half of which we didn't use.

On top at dusk, Vern and I shake hands a little awkwardly. There is no question that we have created the finest route in Tuolumne. Nevertheless, our friendship is precarious, me enmeshed in the work-a-day world and Vern the rebel, defiant of the world below.

As Vern begins down, I stay for a moment, thinking of Tuolumne as my *femme fatale.* Here, years ago, I touched the rock like a boy might first touch a nubile girl, gingerly, unsurely. I went sleepless, turning and re-turning the thought of the next day's rendezvous. I sometimes whistled, like a rowdy, at the billowing shape of the tall, round domes. In the midst of it all, as with a lover, I felt lustful, whole, godly, as well as small and angered. How frequently the nubile child became harsh mistress, whimsical and demanding, though gorgeous still. Often she rewarded us only after we backed away to try again to please her. We were learning and she was teaching. But in the end, she smiled on us like a mother who rewards a certain goodness, so that at the close of recent seasons, I could step from the car on the return drive, look across treetops crisply held in fall air to Fairview, the queen herself, and feel full of thanks.

Below, Vern is a wispy shadow on the gradual slabs. He cannot know how, for me, this splendid route is a virtual consecration of so many walls, days, evening fires, night skies, and a special friendship. Before me, bathing the dome in pale silver, rises the slow moon. Now, in gladness, I finally may say goodbye. ☐

SOUTHEAST ALASKA
FRED BECKEY

THE MOUNTAINS of Southeast Alaska present a formidable, intriguing, and altogether confusing panorama. Such is the complexity of the mountain topography in this region that much of its early history of exploration and political determination reads like a compendium of geographers' errors. The greater region is quite naturally defined, yet it is still perplexing because of the innumerable sub-ranges and river drainages. More confusion results from the political division, since the alpine zone is shared nearly equally by Alaska and Canada.

This article will deal only with that portion of the northern coastal ranges which actually lies within Southeast Alaska or along the border of British Columbia. I will first consider the topography and geology of the mountains; reference to the accompanying map should be helpful. Later, the history of early exploration in this region will be covered. Finally, I will discuss the relatively brief climbing history.

GEOGRAPHY

THE COAST MOUNTAINS of Alaska, whose interior portions extend into Canada, begin at the shores of the Portland Canal—at a latitude of 54°53'—and, as the Boundary Ranges, extend northwest to about the 59th parallel, where they become known as the Alsek Ranges. West of Glacier Bay and the Grand Pacific Glacier, the mountains become the Fairweather Range.

To the north, the Saint Elias Mountains form major elements of the Pacific Mountain System between the latitudes 59° and 62° N and longitudes 137° and 142° W. Rising as a high barrier between the ocean and the continental interior, they comprise a number of roughly parallel ranges which form a shallow arc through nearly 300 miles. In width they span a distance of more than 100 miles between the Gulf of Alaska and the Yukon Plateau.

Mt. Fairweather from the east/*Bradford Washburn*

Their topography is that of a high alpine region with major valleys largely submerged beneath the most extensive mantle of snow and ice in continental North America. The area has been subdivided into several physiographic regions; the highest central core is called the Icefield Ranges.

The equally dramatic, but more compact, Fairweather Range contains no fewer than seven peaks which exceed 12,000 feet in elevation; many surpass 9,000 feet. Largest of them all is Mt. Fairweather, 15,320 feet high. Only twenty-odd miles from the sea, it is barely challenged among the mountains of the world for its massive stature. While both the Icefield and Fairweather ranges could be considered within the domain of Southeast Alaska, only the latter will be included in this article.

The heavy precipitation and snowfall in both the Coast Mountains and the Fairweather Range have resulted in extensive erosion and steep gradients. Complex networks of valley glaciers act as distributory tongues from both high cirques and icefields. Glaciers often flow from icefields over both sides of a divide, then drop down deep valleys, past dense forests, and finally either thrust into intricate systems of fiords or push ice snouts into meltwater lakes. Glacier-dammed lakes are a common phenomenon. When the water rises to float the dam, there are catastrophic outbursts and rapid drainage is inevitable. In the Fairweather Range the Fairweather and Grand Plateau glaciers are the principal iceways to the sea, yet the La Pérouse, a small piedmont glacier, is the only one actually discharging into the open ocean.

When the glaciers of Glacier Bay and Juneau regions were at the position of maximum recession, mature forests grew far up the valleys. These interstadial forests, later buried beneath advancing ice, are now being uncovered by retreat. The most recent advance apparently reached a maximum at the close of the eighteenth century. In Glacier Bay has occurred the greatest recent deglaciation in the world. Pre-glacial terrain features in Southeastern Alaska present incontestable evidence that maximum advance took place a few centuries ago and that recession has subsequently been the general rule. Trimlines were carved in old forests by advancing ice; at a lower level youthful first generation forests occupy land which has been free of ice since the last maximum. On the west side of the Lynn Canal, a series of valley glaciers descend but none reach sea level. A perennial mantle of snow and ice covers the crests of the Taku and Stikine watersheds.

The Taku Glacier, one of eleven large valley glaciers flowing from the 700-square-mile Juneau Icefield, has been advancing for at least a half century. The complex anomalies of adjacent glaciers in states of advance and retreat prompted the American Geographical Society in 1941 to send its first field party to this region. Evidence indicates that in the mid-eighteenth century, the Taku, in coalescence with its neighbor the Norris Glacier, extended across the Taku inlet. Then it receded, but by about 1900 a new advance began; it has continued to the present time. The Taku system interlocks on the vast icefield with the Lewellyn, which flows toward Lake Atlin on the Canadian slope. An associated iceflow, the Twin Glaciers, parades well-developed "Forbes dirt bands." The twisted moraine patterns of some Alaskan glaciers show cases of surging.

The glaciologists Tarr and Martin have mentioned that the glaciers near the Devil's Thumb are the southernmost seen from a steamer, and here the LeConte (latitude 57° N) is the last tidal glacier. Its canyon was called *Hutli*, or Thunder Bay, by the Indians because of the noise made by calving ice. Holkam Bay, with four tidal glaciers in its branches, Tracy and Endicott Arms, was considered by Muir to be one of the most interesting of the fiords. Large valley glaciers exist farther south in the tributaries of the Behm Canal and in the Bear and Salmon River valleys of the Portland Canal; all these no longer reach tidewater.

The Pacific system of mountains does not always have a distinct crestline but is an aggregate of mountain masses which act as a climatic barrier between the sea and the interior. The Coast Mountains drop precipitously into Pacific waters, creating a labyrinth of fiords or drowned glacier valleys which twist into a giant jigsaw of islands hundreds of miles in length. These myriad islands, the Alexander Archipelago, with their vast irregular waterways, represent the actual Coast Range—which dwindles into offshore islands. Some of these mountains are higher at fiord entrances than at their headwaters and present a strange, bold, promontory effect. Beaches are rare. In complete contrast are the interior sub-ranges of the Coast Mountains, where even a major volcano, Mt. Edziza, is located. Here are such groups as the Spectrum Range, which has colorful sedimentary rock layers a few miles from jagged granitic peaks at the eastern margins of the mountains.

Mts. Orville and Wilbur/*Washburn*

Devil's Paw from the northeast/*Austin Post*

Southeast of the Fairweather Range the peaks now most familiar to the public are those of the Juneau Icefield, between Juneau and Atlin Lake (in British Columbia), where the great massif of Devil's Paw is outstanding. South of the Taku River and west of the Stikine River rise Mt. Ratz and its contingent of peaks: Kate's Needle (not visible from the coast), and Devil's Thumb, which was named by Commander R. W. Meade (1869) for its "thumblike projection on the mountain." Kate's Needle, probably named by surveyors on the Stikine river, was not entered on official reports until 1893. Farther east and southeast are a myriad of sub-ranges, the major ones centered about Mounts Hickman, Lewis Cass, and Jancowski, and in the Cambria Icefield. Few of the individual peaks have been identified and few have been climbed. The ranges are nearly unknown except from distant or aerial surveys.

The geology of the Coast Ranges is vastly complex, but it may be noted that they are intruded by a composite granitic batholith nearly one thousand miles long—one of the world's greatest plutonic masses. East of the great fault through Chatham Strait and Lynn Canal, the batholith was intruded in Cretaceous time, accompanied by great crustal compression, and this was greatly folded and sheared before the ice sculpturing in Pleistocene and Recent times. The bedrock, once deeply buried in the crust, then uplifted, follows an orientation parallel to the axis of the Alaska Panhandle. A wide spectrum of sedimentary and metamorphic formations occurs along the batholith margins.

The tenacity of these hard, granitic-type rocks to stream and glacial erosion is the main reason for their jagged form, a consistency that is evident the entire length of the ranges. The Fairweather Range contains young mountains, and they owe much of their height to dramatic uplifts during the Pleistocene and Recent times. It is claimed that in this short period of the geologic time scale they rose as much as 5,000 feet. Slippage along the Fairweather and Denali faults is not rare. During the tremendous earthquake of 1958, ninety million tons of rock broke loose above Lituya Bay and caused a surging wave that boiled water to a height of 1,720 feet, stripping forest and shore in a great natural catastrophe.

Apprehensive as man is to such unpredictable forces, the more immediate problems in the Coast Mountains are forests, brush, and glaciers. The boggy spruce and hemlock forests in the deeper valleys and near the coast can provide exasperating obstacles to foot travel. The understory is perhaps the most difficult in the world to penetrate, and it features the malevolent devil's club (*Echinopanax horrida*), which grows to a height of eight feet along streams and valley bottoms.

The mountain belt is characterized by a wet, cold climate on the slopes that face the Gulf of Alaska and coastal waterways, and by a dry, cold, even semi-arid, climate in the continental interior. Records show an annual precipitation of 125 inches beneath the Fairweather Range, while at Telegraph Creek, on the eastern scarp, the annual precipitation is not over 20 inches. The northward migration of a Pacific High can bring warm daytime temperatures to the coastal regions, but the summer patterns become complicated when the Aleutian Low migrates into and out of the Gulf of Alaska. The month of May can still be very wintery, but June is usually a transition month in Alaskan mountains. Though general conditions are a good deal warmer in August, storms can be much more violent and of much longer duration than in early summer. Bradford Washburn summarizes the situation: "Dramatic spring temperatures change in early June with less wind and cold but continual snow showers. The winter snow results in slush and avalanches. At the end of June, weather stabilizes more with some bad storms, but often clear weather above 6,000 feet and seas of clouds below that. During June and July it will snow as low as 5,000 feet and rarely rains above 6,000 feet. In August these seas of clouds diminish, the southwesters shift to southeast storms, and it isn't unlikely that you will have rain as high as 11,000 feet."

EXPLORATION

ON HIS THIRD world voyage, in 1778, Captain James Cook first saw Mt. Fairweather as a "very high peaked mountain." This he entered on charts as Mount Fair Weather among "mountains...wholly covered with snow from the highest summit down to the sea coast." But Cook did not approach the coast closely, for he was searching for the Straits of Annian, portrayed as a feature of North America on Jonathan Swift's fanciful 1740 map. The British government had finally been aroused to collect definite information and not rely wholly on the Hudson Bay Company's explorations.

Captain Tebenkof of the Imperial Russian Navy made the first coherent charts of these mountains; they showed a single line of ridges. At the same time he called attention to Alaskan glaciers and reported that icebergs floated all summer in Icy Strait. Tebenkof showed respect for the dangers at Lituya Bay: "Nothing disturbs the deep silence of this terribly grand gorge of the mountains but the thunder of falling icebergs." Tebenkof apparently did not go ashore to explore the glaciers, but in a later report stated that logbooks showed that Russian vessels had sent explorers in 1788 to follow the shoreline of Icy Bay.

During his visit to the Fairweather Range in 1786, the French explorer Comte de La Pérouse lost two boatloads of men at the treacherous entrance of Lituya Bay, the harbor of early Russian seal hunters. His party actually advanced two leagues onto the Lituya Glacier, making probably the first glacier exploration in these regions. French maps and texts later showed Mt. Crillon, Mt. Dagelet, Mt. La Pérouse; Mt. Fairweather was indicated as *Beautems* or *Beau-temps*.

Captain George Vancouver, in 1794, showed the Fairweather Range on his charts. In a marvel of accomplishment that made his maps the accredited ones for over one hundred years, Vancouver accurately charted the confusing coastal shores and islands for a distance of 700 miles; his charts depicted a continuous mountain chain running around the heads of all inlets. About the time of his visit the most recent glacial advance apparently was reaching a maximum. At Glacier Bay he noted the bay and entrance: "The shores of the continent form two large, open bays, which were terminated by compact, solid mountains of ice rising perpendicularly from the water's edge and bounded to the north by a continuation of the united, lofty, frozen mountains that extend eastward from Mount Fairweather." Vancouver and his crew were continually impressed with "the stupendous snowy barrier rising from the sea abruptly to the clouds," and a peak near the Baird Glacier inspired a subordinate to report that "the mountains rose abruptly to a prodigious height...loaded with an immense quantity of ice and snow, and overhanging their base."

There were other expeditions, more land-oriented. In 1877, Lt. C.E.S. Wood and Charles Taylor were prevented from making an exploration to the Mt. Saint Elias region by a mutiny of native boatmen; an old chief pointed to Mt. Fairweather and said, "One mountain is as good as another. There is a very big one. Go, climb that, if you want to." Wood returned to cross the divide northeast of Fairweather with a party of goat hunters; he found much game, including the silver-tipped bear.

In 1869 the Chilkat chief Kloh-kutz told Professor George Davidson about a bay full of breaking ice cliffs. Lying west of Lynn Canal, it was only a day's journey by snowshoe, and he urged the professor to make the journey with him and watch the hair-seals riding on ice floes and the ice rumbling like landslides into the water. Davidson, who prepared the intricate Coast and Geodetic Survey charts, mapped the peaks and glaciers of the Fairweather Range and Coast Mountains so thoroughly that he became the expert on boundary matters for the United States. He felt that the Brady Glacier emanated from an extensive *mer de glacé* and that it was positively advancing.

William P. Blake examined the glaciers of the Stikine River in 1863 and discovered that in Tlingit legends evil spirits devoured canoe occupants. He wrote, "it was impossible to get an Indian guide to accompany us." Apparently the Indians had a tradition of the loss of one of their chiefs on the Great Glacier. Based on the Russian corvette *Rynda*, Blake made careful descriptions of the Stikine glaciers. He wrote of his problems crossing a glacier: "The surface soon became precipitous and broken into irregular stair-like blocks with smooth sides...impossible to make our way over them without ladders." Blake noted that the chain of the Coast Mountains "is seen to be lofty and alpine in character...sharply serrated, and...here and there into needle-like pinnacles."

John Muir made similar observations in 1879 from the summit of Glenora Peak, shortly after the Stikine became an important artery to the placer gold mines of the Cassiar region. Muir counted 300 glaciers in the area and in Glacier Bay revealed his enchantment: "Northeastward of Fairweather innumerable white peaks are displayed, the highest fountainheads of the Muir Glacier crowded together in bewildering array." Muir landed to observe the La Pérouse Glacier overwhelming forests (confirmed twenty years later by the Harriman Expedition) and noted the vast recession at Glacier Bay between his and an earlier Vancouver visit: Johns Hopkins Inlet had formed and the Grand Pacific Glacier had become three independent tidal glaciers. But Muir found the bay full of floating ice, as native seal hunters had told him. With a companion and Indians he canoed to the head of the bay and later brought his knowledge to the world. Eliza Scidmore felt that Muir is justly entitled to the honor as the discoverer of Glacier Bay. Scidmore also made many studies of these glaciers and cast new light on two Russians who had disappeared earlier on the Great (Orlebar) Glacier. "Two young Russian officers once came down from Sitka to explore it, but never returned from their expedition, and prospectors are said to have been lost in its crevasses."

Scidmore made an early observation of Kate's Needle: "its dark summit pricked sharply through snow-fields to the very sky...in some far recess near there hides that mysterious Flood Glacier, which several times each season breaks away a natural dam and sends a torrent of muddy water roaring out to the river."

Kate's Needle/*Dick Culbert*

Stikine peaks/*Post*

The present Alaska-Canada frontier appears to be largely the result of the 1827 map of A.J. de Krusenstern, the Russian admiral and navigator. His map showed the frontier of Russian America beginning at the head of the Portland Canal, following the coastal sinuousities northward at a distance of ten marine leagues inland, and then heading north on the 141st meridian. Captain Vancouver adopted the general features of the Russian maps; subsequent mapmakers and diplomats came to regard the supposed single mountain chain as a natural and proper boundary. The later claims of the United States against Canada were based on an old treaty with Russia which took this map-made, crooked line along summits to Mt. Saint Elias. Later explorations proved, of course, that there was no concise mountain chain and no dominant ridgeline, only a sea of mountains. *La crète des montagnes* (the crest of the mountains) of La Pérouse, on which the Boundary Tribunal based its decisions, was largely an illusion.

Various maps went through a series of transformations regarding the boundary. After the United States purchased Alaska in 1867, the vague boundary needed accurate determination. It was soon shown that there was no definite watershed division within ten marine leagues of the coast. Not until 1906 (long after the problem was submitted to the Boundary Tribunal) did the Canadian and American governments send field parties into the region to determine once and for all the exact position of the frontier. Thus began one of the heroic sagas of mountain exploration, a still largely unheralded chapter in the history of exploratory mountaineering. The deeds of these surveyors are shrouded in anonymity since government agencies were (and are) inclined to limit data to mere statistics in the official accounts. Thus, many of their accomplishments may never be known. For example, in 1895 a Canadian survey party mapped Glacier Bay and the Alsek Glacier, but it is not known what peaks they may have climbed.

The basic task was to survey and mark a 600-mile border from the Portland Canal to the 141st meridian and to cut twenty-foot vistas in the timbered valleys. All this had to be done in short field seasons. Provisional maps used by the Alaska Boundary Tribunal in 1903 were to determine which peaks were to become boundary points, but due to vast gaps in knowledge, these were not necessarily the highest or even most important peaks. Yet the surveyors still had to climb those summits within their capabilities, then determine the elevations of the others geodetically. Log rafts had to be built for river ferrying and swamps had to be crossed. Provisions had to be placed in elevated caches, laboriously constructed so as to be safe from animal marauders. Heavy topographic cameras and theodolites had to be carried up brushy, cliff-laced mountain slopes and across icefields. On the Dawes Glacier a survey party took eight hours to travel four miles. And often these surveyors saved each other by use of the rope, or by throwing an alpenstock across hidden, collapsing crevasses or snow bridges. East of Endicott Arm, in the survey season of 1909, a man fell 2,000 feet.

A Canadian field party on the Taku River in 1906 identified and named the Devil's Paw. Led by W.F. Ratz, the party ascended Tallsaykway (now Tulsequah) River to its glacier. In 1910 they climbed this outlet valley glacier to the vast icefields and climbed Boundary Peak 94.

In 1907 field parties spent the summer mapping out of Glacier Bay. In part this was due to the importance of Mounts Fairweather and Root as boundary points. Again, it is uncertain that alpine achievements were accomplished. During the same year a Canadian party on the Stikine River ascended to a 7,300-foot point northwest of Kate's Needle. Ratz penned a legend for the nearby Devil's Thumb: "a high sugarloaf peak." In 1908 the surveyors found the Dawes Glacier very difficult of travel and used sleds for transport.

MOUNTAINEERING

THE HIGHEST MOUNTAINS in many ranges are often the first climbed, primarily because of their compelling attraction. There are many peaks more difficult to climb in Southeast Alaska than Mt. Fairweather, but none demanded greater effort and fortitude to scale originally.

The two-month-long exploit of Allen Carpé, Andy Taylor, William Ladd, and Terris Moore on Mt. Fairweather in the early summer of 1931 ranks as one of the rare stories in the annals of North American mountaineering. They had little benefit from the attempt of 1926, because the Ladd-Carpé-Taylor party of that year had attempted the west ridge, only to halt at a deep cleft at 9,100 feet. In 1930 Bradford Washburn's expedition, which began from Lituya Bay, did not even reach this obstacle. The 1931 group determined to attempt the mountain from the south.

Lituya Bay was again the natural base of operations. The party advanced up the Fairweather Glacier, then set camps on the chosen rib of the mountain. Because of the short duration of good weather spells, they had to climb in stages. Climbing into a storm, the team made a summit attempt that had to be halted. Almost out of food, Taylor and Ladd descended; a cold, clear day permitted Carpé and Moore to make the summit. From the top they could see the coast like a chart. Such dramatic vistas are just one of the rewards of climbing in these immense mountains.

The climb was repeated by a Canadian party in 1958, and two members of the party, Fips Broda and Walter Romanes, climbed the challenging Mt. Sabine nearby. The Fairweather Range has seen successful climbs since then, notably Dave Bohn's party's ascents of Mt. Lituya, Mt. Quincy Adams, Mt. Watson, Fairweather's west ridge, its southwest ridge, and the traverse of its east ridge via Quincy Adams.

Mt. Crillon from the northwest/*Washburn*

Mt. La Pérouse from the southwest/*Washburn*

Mt. Crillon proved an enigma before being climbed in 1934 by Bradford Washburn and Adams Carter. Washburn's 1933 expedition deserved the climb, for they succeeded in reaching the vexing upper plateau and were only defeated by violent weather at the false summit. Washburn's expeditions, science-oriented and heavily laden, were limited to a slow pace. The first ascent of Mt. Bertha, which Washburn approached from Glacier Bay, smacked of traditional Alaskan mountaineering, for the expedition used dogs for sledding. Using an entirely different and modern philosophy of going light and fast, Dusan Jagersky and Larry Nielson made a new route on Mt. Bertha in 1972. However, some of the stylistic purity of this ascent (and their face-climbs on Mt. La Pérouse) vanishes when it is learned that the ascents were helicopter supported from a mining expedition legally operating within Glacier Bay National Monument. The logistics and risks taken by the pioneers who began at tidewater, without air support, seem vast by comparison.

Here is a philosophic dilemma, for the Monument's superintendent does not allow mountaineering airdrops or landings, yet the potential excavators play noisybird, flying anywhere for both fun and profit as they anticipate shipping the Fairweather Range to Japan.

The magnificent peak of Crillon was not climbed again until the summer of 1972, this time via the west ridge. This ascent was made by a party of Alaskans: Loren Adkins, Marsha Adkins, Bruce Tickell, Dick Benedict, and Jerry Buckley.

Mt. La Pérouse has seen what are probably the hardest technical climbs in the Fairweather Range since its first ascent by a U.S. Geological Survey party in 1952. In 1959 Leo Scheiblehner and a companion climbed a steep, 7,000-foot-high face on the east peak, solving a difficult problem as well as being the first to reach the summit. The northeast ridge and north face was climbed in 1972 by Dusan Jagersky and Larry Nielson; it was a long, hard, icy climb done in a twenty-hour push.

Mt. Burkett and Devil's Thumb/*Post*

The Takhinsha Mountains, west of Haines, were explored by Larry Nielson's party in 1966. While they did not climb the highest summit, they reached the second highest. Though these mountains are not very high, they are formidable because they rise from near sea level. Nielson has undertaken other explorations in the little-known ranges between the Fairweather and Juneau regions; in 1968 his group did pioneer climbing in the Chilkoot Range, southeast of Skagway.

The Indians called the Taku Glacier *Sitth Klummu Gutta.* Father Bernard Hubbard interpreted this as "Spirit's Home," and, after his 1927 visits to the icefields from both the Mendenhall Glacier and Twin Glacier Lake, wrote, "closing in the majestic sight the towering sawtooth mountains of the Coast Range rise like Gothic spires."

Recognizing the area's unique value for research, the American Geographical Society, in 1948, formed plans for the Juneau Icefield Research Project. Under the leadership of Maynard Miller, this program has developed into an extensive, permanent field facility for academic and practical training in the polar and glacial sciences. The network of field camps has given bases from which to climb many of the surrounding peaks. The ski crossing of the icefield from the Twin Glaciers to the Mendenhall in 1949 was purely mountaineering-oriented. The craggy hulk of the Devil's Paw yielded to Bill Putnam, Dave Michael, and Andy Griscom; its spectacular rock satellite, Michael's Sword, was climbed by Fred Beckey and Harry King. The highest of the Mendenhall Towers was climbed by Stuart Wilson and a companion in the 1950s. The striking towers of this region have seen recent technical rockclimbing by John Svenson and others. Members of the glacier research project climbed the attractive Higher Taku Tower in the 1950s, but the lower tower was not ascended until the recent, technical east face route of Dan Reid's party. Blade-like Horn Spire, near the Gilkey Glacier north of Juneau, was climbed in 1973 by the Lingle-Bickell-Benedict-Buckley party, a year after the Beckey-Rupley-Beckstead climb of the Tusk.

The great ice peak of Kate's Needle was investigated by Fritz Wiessner and Bestor Robinson in 1937, but little is known of their trip except that they encountered more rain than climbing. In the summer of 1946 Wiessner joined Fred Beckey for another expedition via the Flood Glacier, but a knee injury forced Wiessner to retire. Clifford Schmidtke, Bob Craig, and Beckey continued the plan and, after much relaying of loads, climbed the peak via the north face in a twenty-four-hour round trip from their camp. One of their camps was ravaged of food supplies during their absence, but their resources were sufficient to allow them to continue on skis across the icefield divide to the Devil's Thumb. Frustrating weather forced back several attempts, but the difficult summit was finally reached on the last possible day which would allow them to make the weekly river boat on the Stikine.

The Canadian threesome of Dick Culbert, Paul Starr, and Fred Douglas adventured into this region twice; in 1970 they reported the climb of the Devil's Thumb via the direct east ridge. Then, two years later, they climbed the sensational Cat's Ears; this ascent required two bivouacs. Concurrently, during a spell of settled weather, Beckey, Rupley, and Beckstead were making the first ascent of Mt. Hickman, the highest mountain east of the Stikine River. In this very unexplored sector, an earlier Seattle-based group had climbed Mt. Ambition.

The Stikine Icefield was visited in 1964, when three important summits were climbed: Mt. Ratz by Beckey and Dan Davis, Mt. Mussell by Henryk Mather and Layton Kor, and the Burkett Needle by Kor and Davis. A Scottish expedition in 1966 made a number of climbs, including the first ascent of Mt. Burkett, and the second ascent of Kate's Needle. The most ambitious undertaking, in generally stormy conditions, took place in 1973 when George Lowe, Chris Jones, and Lito Tejada-Flores climbed the impressive southeast face of the Devil's Thumb. This was probably the most miserable as well as technically difficult episode in the Boundary Ranges.

The Cat's Ears from the Devil's Thumb/*George Lowe*

THE FUTURE of Southeast Alaska and its forests, fiords, and mountains is uncertain from the standpoint of environmental protection and economic development. J. A. Bancroft long ago urged the government to reserve several of the most picturesque fiords as parks, a dream that hopefully may become a reality.

The weather-battered environment of these ranges is one of complete isolation. Hikers and climbers will not find here the traditions and facilities of the Alps, and they would do well to evaluate carefully both motives and objectives. Self-reliance, self-support and good judgement, perhaps more than in most mountain ranges, are prime requisites. Most of the people living in the coastal or island towns have no interest in the ranges, much less in mountaineering. But for those who seek raw adventure, the future of Southeast Alaska is full of promise. It is indeed a land of utmost challenge, individual initiative, and lonely beauty. □

Illustrations by Allison Clough

POONTANGA
GEOFFREY CHILDS

The Humboltkin Letters, of which this journal is comprised, are viewed by many knowledgeable observers of mountaineering as a major discovery, not only in terms of what they represent as the documentation of a great adventure, but for what they have added to the store of twentieth century literature. Many consider the collection to be an instant classic. As in all great writing, the author has captured history and given us a very remarkable character and made both live in our minds. The event, of course, is the long-debated confirmation of Poontanga's first ascent; the character, himself—David Humboltkin.

In editing these pages for publication, extensive research was carried out so as to leave no doubt in anyone's mind as to the authenticity of the journal. Both the penmanship and style of the original manuscript have been identified by friends and members of the late climber's family as his own. As if in final documentation of this fact, roommates of his from the University of Colorado, where Humboltkin first became seriously involved in the study of Poontanga, have begun a scholarship trust in his name based solely on the explorer's wishes as expressed in these pages. It is a tribute to him that his friends have been virtually overwhelmed by the number of young candidates showing "an active and vital interest in developing his approach to Poontanga." From what one is able to gather about the man, this healthy and growing interest in his field would have made Humboltkin deeply happy. As he implies time and again, he sought Poontanga not just for himself, but to show others the way.

Here is the journal then, with no further comment other than to simply ask that you attempt to understand the enormity of the undertaking before you judge the author for his all too human weaknesses.

                1 September 1959
                The Khomanghettit Glacier

I have dreamed during most of my adult life of someday standing in this exact spot. In truth, I have seen myself standing here since before I even knew such a place existed beyond a boy's wildest caprice. Yet since 1956, when the expedition began to take the shape of destiny, I have made this adventure—this mountain—my life. In other moments I have composed a thousand pages of prose to describe the sights and feelings I imagined I would experience upon first viewing the incredible beauty that would lie before me. And yet now that I am here seeing and feeling those things, I can find no words! How much greater my understanding is now of Sir Twillingbyrd-Smythe's having trod this same ground and only being able to utter, "formica...formica...."

The panorama seems to overwhelm the sad paucity of the English language. Only the broadest and most hopeless descriptions apply. To the south the vast, mile-thick, gray carpet of the monsoon covers the entire mass of the Indian subcontinent; to my right and to my left and always above me are the mountains! They are impossibly beautiful; frightening and at the same time alluring; impassive and yet sensual beyond resisting. And there in their midst, spreading out ridges toward us as if welcoming the challenge, is Poontanga!

The traditional approach to climbing her has proven to be as theoretically sound and realistically ineffective as traditional answers usually are. No doubt it is the sensible route, the ultimately rational line; it assumes the obvious and exploits the apparent weaknesses of the mountain. But it will not go. Twillingbyrd-Smythe's ill-starred British attempt decided that conclusively. While they were able to easily overcome the initial problems of Poontanga's twin guardian peaks to the north—Hoon-kee and Do-ree—the expedition floundered and was eventually turned back by the incredible complexities involved in traversing the Plain of Snows. Poontanga, it seems, does not reward subtleness with conquest; she waits to be taken boldly! Thus will we be taking the more dangerous, more technically demanding line up the west leading leg called 'Idareya' by the natives. A bold thrust along this inside line, if executed with calm and courage and timing, should deliver us our goal, but we do not expect it to come easily.

As has already been well publicized, our team is an international one. Besides me, we are two Serbians, an Afghan, a Croatian dwarf, an unemployed fortune-teller named Friggo, whose place of origin is unknown, a Viennese, and our three faithful Sherpas, Hui, Doui, and Loui. Much has been made of the fact that no international expedition has ever successfully climbed a major Himalayan peak. Failure in almost every case has been attributed

to problems of leadership and accepting responsibility. We feel we have prepared for this and will hopefully overcome it by assembling a team entirely lacking any sense of responsibility or interest in leading anything.

But enough about us. Tomorrow before dawn we begin climbing! I will diligently try to maintain this journal to the best of my ability, until we have either reached the top or suffered whatever else chance has in store for us.

7 September 1959
Camp II—Ghettin Klosar Glacier

Camp II has been established and we are in the process of investigating sites for advance camps along the ridge. Apart from the daily drudgery of trekking down to Camp I and then back up, life here takes on a routine of its own. One has to prod himself to acknowledge the staggeringly beautiful scenery surrounding us. We settle into our own formulas: I write, Lkjhgfdski—the Serbian—seems content to be constantly scrubbing out his underwear; Lobisa, a prince in his native Afghanistan, toys with his pet spiders, and our Sherpas are happy to spend their spare time sitting in a small circle passing around a pipe filled with some loathsome-smelling native tobacco which, despite its bizarre stench, only seems to enhance their remarkable cheerfulness!

As the critical moments of the climb seem to be yet in front of us, now seems an appropriate time to take a moment and deal with some of the criticism that has so long surrounded our choice of Dr. Armando Flies as physician. As you will doubtless recall, there was a great deal of open skepticism in some quarters where it was felt his background in animal vasectomy was inadequate to our needs. I will not honor that kind of thinking by calling it controversy. Since having joined us in Calcutta, Armo (as he is affectionately referred to) has endeared himself to all of us as a companion, and his performance in the field of medicine has been thoroughly professional and, at times, even superhuman. I hope it will put to rest all doubts of his ability if I say that without him and his remarkable medications, the expedition would surely have been doomed. Apart from the typically wide range of bruises and lacerations he has had to contend with, he has also willingly taken on the additional burden of our spiritual and psychic health. Perhaps our greatest single debt to him lies therein. I myself remember having gone to him once after an especially long day's trek and blurting out a dream I had had in which I saw myself as a goldfish being swallowed alive by a fraternity boy from Colgate. How clearly I recall the doctor's laughing, placing a comforting hand on my shoulder and explaining that, "dreams are simply a sign that everything is well with the subconscious and that the ego is getting the input it needs."

While God has seen fit to keep us from serious injury, we are victims, like all other Himalayan explorers, of the effects of altitude. Yet Dr. Flies' daily examinations of climbers returning from the high camps have so far prevented anyone from developing hair on their palms or writing crude letters to the governor of Indiana. The amazing ration of golden, crystal-like powder he discovered while shopping for medication in Katmandu has been the mission's greatest success story. Inhaled through either nostril on a regular basis, it miraculously eliminates the headaches and colds so frequent above 17,000 feet, not to mention what it has done for our morale, the way it has stabilized our blood pressure, spared us the discomfort of having to eat, and saved us from the heartbreak of psoriasis.

Tomorrow we will be moving into the monolithic blue ice folds of the upper Odsyen Glacier. At this time of year the ice seracs overhang one another like huge vaults, building and growing sodden with wet snow until finally they collapse. I would be less than realistic to believe that the possibility of death was not concealed therein and less than fair if I were to risk a premature ending to these pages without first thanking some of those who made the expedition fact. While it was our desire to draw financial support from as many sources as possible and thereby remain a "people's expedition," special thanks are still called for. Our greatest thanks, then, must go to Vice-President Nixon for his words of encouragement (we will leave his shoes on the summit!) and to the owners of the Broadway Deli, Sid and Erma Goldman for their contribution of a life-sized swan made entirely from raw chicken livers.

17 September 1959
Camp II

Snow squalls these past ten days have made any movement up impossible. Most of every waking hour is spent melting snow for tea, kicking spindrift from the roof of the tent, and occasionally peering outside for a glimpse of anything resembling a break in the weather. Nights are spent tossing and turning in our sleeping sacks. Dfghjkin, the Serbian, and I have tried playing chess—that is, I have attempted to teach him a few of the game's more refined gambits—but he has proven hopeless as an opponent. Lobisa claims this is because he clubbed Dfghjkin two days ago following a misunderstanding over some Serbian after-dinner ritual which Lobisa construed to be an uncalled-for commentary on his ability to cook baked beans. This certainly would explain the Serbian's stalling tactics after my having cleverly maneuvered him into check yesterday afternoon. Nevertheless, I consider his attitude most unsportsmanlike and probably one of the reasons these international things never get off the ground.

Our Sherpas continue to function extremely well. Much has been made recently of a so-called demise in both their willingness and ability to serve. If this is true, I have personally seen no sign of it. I have read report after report blaming them for this or that mission's failure to achieve its intended goal. Explanations of this phenomenon seem inevitably to take the form of sociological treatises illuminating the "rapid changes manifest in the Sherpa society" due to the advent of large but poorly distributed sums of currency. Money, it has been alleged, and not the mountains has become the central life-force of the once noble Sherpa. I can only brand this sort of agonizing as utter rubbish! In the most purely subjective of terms, my relationship with the darkies has been superb. They have been consistently helpful and courageous, treating us with both hospitality and deference. They are open, unsophisticated, and cherishing. They respond to strength with strength, and if the summit falls to us, the burden of credit belongs to them. Indeed, the memory of this expedition which will outlast all others is that of our last night in

a Sherpa hamlet before our climb. Totally to our surprise we were invited to take part in a native ceremony as old as their culture itself. In an ageless gesture of parting and farewell we were given local trinkets in exchange for our American Express Checks (the poor fools, they were fascinated by the colors). Later, sitting in one of our guide's home watching television, the Sherpa confessed to us that as soon as his son returned from Oxford, he was thinking about moving to the Middle East, where he had heard the climate was kinder and money was to be made in oil. Sadly, there was no explaining to him the genetic inability of the Arab to fully exploit this natural resource.

19 September 1959
Camp II

Snow continues to fall, though the sun broke through for a short time today and portends better weather on the morrow. Lkjhgfdski and I will leave at dawn and attempt to establish Camp III. Morale remains high, particularly since Myerbeck, the Viennese, announced his engagement to his right hand. The simple ceremony left us all deeply moved, and a bottle of champagne intended for our post-climb celebration was opened for a toast. Bashful as ever, Myerbeck quietly admitted that they had no formal plans for their future yet, though they had discussed buying a house trailer and moving to Argentina, where he has friends from "the old days."

21 September 1959
Camp III

Camp III having been quickly established in a huge snow cavern beneath an outward jutting mass of rock, we are about to begin the climb toward the knoll on the edge of the plateau called the Knee. We are carrying enough equipment to place Camp IV should luck be with us. Its projected altitude would be just over 23,000 feet, higher than any of us have ever been before. Thanks to Dr. Flies, we seem to be acclimatizing well, and life at 18,800 feet above sea level has certainly proved to have its own oddities. Our moods tend to alter radically without explanation. The feeling of all-consuming lethargy absorbs every thought and gesture. At times merely getting out of one's sleeping sack becomes an unimaginably difficult task. It is so easy to allow oneself the continuing pleasure of sleep. Myerbeck and Friggo arrived in camp today, greatly improving our morale. Even Lkjhgfdski, who has stayed in his tent talking to his teddy bear for the last three days, was laughing in no time over their hysterical antics. They really are awfully jolly fellows! Only this morning we found them outside their tent, stark naked, holding hands, laughing like fools, dancing the Tarentella, and swatting each other with wet gym towels! I was lucky enough to snap several photos of this which I shall forward along with my article to *National Geographic*.

28 September 1959
Camp IV

After an epic seven-day struggle we have finalized Camp IV. The weather seems to be changing again for the worse. We thought we had been overtaken by the tempest last night, in fact, but the howling and whining proved to be nothing more than Friggo suffering from having over-eaten boiled "thouc," a local specialty prepared with yak dung and small pebbles.

2 October 1959
Camp V

Tragedy has marred the conclusion of our first month on the mountain. Lobisa, accompanied by the three Sherpas, set out yesterday to find a location for Camp VI. They had already negotiated their way though the major difficulties when they were overtaken by a storm. For eight hours they continued climbing, struggling like men possessed, determined to either succeed in establishing a sixth camp or perish in the effort. At 7:30 p.m., in near complete darkness, with the storm swirling around them, they grappled over the edge of a small platform beside an ice gully and elected to bivouac there. Unfortunately, the platform was already the site of Camp IV which they had somehow circumnavigated. The misfortune was further compounded when in the morning it was discovered that in seeking to find a solid anchor for a guy-line, one of the Sherpas, crazed and half-blind with exhaustion, seems to have driven a snow stake through Lkjhgfdski, who was squatting in the snow.

A great deal of debate has naturally followed our finding his body frozen into the ice this morning, some feeling that he should be removed to a lower base for burial and others explaining that the validity of the route depended upon his being left in place as he had been used as a natural anchor.

12 October 1959
Camp V

We have completed our chain of high camps along the entire length of the Idareya Leg of Poontanga. From the entrance of my tent I can look up and see the smooth, distinctly shaped summit mount. As drawn and soul-spent as the higher camps make one feel, the nearness of the peak still stirs the heart. Victory finds its way into letters and images. Tomorrow, provided the weather holds, four of us will try to turn those words and dreams into reality.

At a moment like this the mind automatically wanders back to other attempts. To the northeast I can clearly make out the broad, flat expanse of the Plain of Snows, guarded on its upper reaches by the jug-shaped masses of Hoon-kee and Do-ree. The route of the British expedition led by Twillingbyrd-Smythe is clearly visible. The point where they were turned back, a location made famous by the French and called the "Nombril," shows itself as a dank, almost circular indentation. Above it the snows are crosshatched in darkness and shadows by slashing, wind-blown lines. No doubt the approach from the north has the subtlety the French appreciate and the quality of propriety the British find so compelling, but I am more convinced than ever that success with Poontanga demands an entirely unique style. The recent Italian effort proved that boldness is not, of itself, enough. Surely it is a prerequisite, but it must be tempered with wisdom and patience. If nothing else is gained by our trial, it is my fondest hope that this new approach will be understood and put to use by tomorrow's young people!

Friggo and Myerbeck have pushed on to establish Camp VI. The additional loads required to support a summit push will be ferried up this afternoon. If all goes well and according to plan, the summit could be ours by the fifteenth!

22 October 1959
Camp VI

It has snowed almost continuously since our arrival at Camp VI nearly ten days ago. Movement of any kind is impossible. We have rationed our food to the point where hunger nags incessantly, making any semblance of sound sleep out of the question. Dozing and dazed awakening seem to run into one another without defination; there is little or no talk, only groans that come out of stupors and stomachs. We are kept between day and night by the clouds. We are urinating into cups inside our sleeping bags to avoid the unbearable cold outside. Lobisa is a pumpkin, Marco. Dear wonderful Marco. If the Lord Mayor could only have known you as a wheel! I have the strangest desire to eat raw oysters. . . .

26 October 1959
Camp VI

And now Madness!! Friggo and Myerbeck deserted camp today during a short respite in the storm. We begged them not to; we warned them, cajoled them, reasoned with them, threatened them physically, and even went so far as to offer them engraved belly-button ornaments if they would only stay. All to no avail. Myerbeck said he was "just going to run down and order a Quarter Pounder with Cheese, an order of fries, a Coke, and change back from his dollar." Then, he claimed, he would return. Friggo, whose teeth were still buried in Myerbeck's thigh, said nothing. The poor, brave fools! The storm engulfed them before they even reached the ropes. Beyond any doubt they are lost. Lobisa and I have withdrawn into our private misery. Occasionally our eyes will meet, then dart to some safe corner of the tent where there is no danger of contact. I have been watching him all morning and he is undoubtedly insane. As I write he is nibbling at his boots, which, I am certain, he thinks is very clever, but which I personally find repugnant.

27 October 1959
Camp VI

We awoke this morning to a perfectly clear, windless day. It brought with it some good news and some bad news. The good news is that Loui, the Sherpa leader, was able to struggle his way through chest-deep snow to bring us a supply of much-needed food. The bad news is that Lobisa was in no state to deal with such emotion, cracked like a china cup and ate the entire contents of Loui's pack. This, of course, has left Lobisa in no condition to climb. I will send him down as soon as he is fit lest he devour the tent in my absence. The final push for Poontanga I shall make myself.

28 October 1959
Camp VI

The weather is again clear. I have sent Lobisa down. The time has come to climb. I am alone in perfect serenity and yet unable to organize my thoughts. Still, the animal sense of having come to a point of no return makes me go through the moves of preparation. I will carry this journal with me to the summit in the event that I am unable to return myself. It will remain there as a testament of my success. Strangely, I am reminded of the Bard's words:

> Liveth doth, men that might be, Alive,
> Extravagence of His master work, how right;
> Shall His fabled strength could hither lead,
> Seed and Loam, Thine smallest movement could bend.

Unfortunately, David Humboltkin was able to make only one more entry in his journal. The handwriting would seem to indicate that his fingers were frozen at the time. It is theorized that Humboltkin reached the summit field of Poontanga shortly after dark. Realizing that it was futile to attempt the descent to Camp VI in the dark, he instead chose to seek shelter in the Pinnacle Crack. It is unlikely that once inside he ever left. His mental state had, in all likelihood, degenerated by this time to the point where he was no longer able to reason effectively, thus accounting for this last, terse entry: "I, Humboltkin, forfmit all imsurance benmfits, should I survive, to rumb MM with rawm garmlic."

It is hard at this time to place his triumph in its proper historical perspective. Humboltkin was thirty-seven years old when he reached Poontanga; nowadays, with all our myriad techniques and sociological pressures, it is not unusual to find fifteen-year-olds doing what Humboltkin did. Sadly, with Poontanga being so much more accessible to everyone these days, it is no longer possible to feel what that great mountaineer/explorer must have felt upon finally realizing his life-long ambition. Poontanga was, at long last, his! As we must admire his courage and daring, so too must we envy him that moment of exultation that few of us are ever privileged to experience. □

SONGS OF THE VERTICAL DESERT
GORDON WILTSIE

LEADERSHIP
HARVEY MANNING

LEADERS HAVE a different look from followers. They get it sometime while being potty-trained or tumbling around a kindergarten playroom. Once they get it, they have it always. People who don't get it early never do.

Leaders have different heads from followers. Ditto.

Followers don't have the look. If they masquerade as leaders, they yell and bully, thinking that will make up for the lack of look. Followers don't have the head. They make bold decisions, thinking that will make up for the lack of thinking. Followers-become-leaders, false leaders, are hermaphrodites despised universally, by none more than themselves.

Deliberately or otherwise, climbing schools insinuate that leading is more admirable than following and thus spawn false leaders. This is particularly so of a school staffed by unpaid volunteers, perpetuated through the principle of "each one teach one." Putting back into the school what one has taken out is a moral imperative. Climbers seeming to have the capacity to lead are expected to do so, are scoundrels if they don't. Because true leaders are rare, false leaders are manufactured in wholesale lots. Frequently to the regret of all.

Consider, for example, the first climb I led for the Climbing Course, Mt. Garfield. A half-hour from the cars we ran into a cliff. A true leader would have chosen the quick and simple end run. I bravely led my twenty-five followers directly into the cliff, up a gully which briefly in the wake of melting glaciers had been a clean gash in the granite, a series of fifty-foot walls broken by neat little chimneys, but these thousands of years later was a vintage low-elevation Cascades mix of brush, dirt, gravel, and rotten logs.

The unroped party was strung out over several hundred vertical feet when we heard a plaintive call, "Help! Help!" Investigation revealed that Bill, disliking my trashy gully, had attempted the naked cliff. He was spreadeagled, fingers quivering, knees doing the sewing machine.

I was about to send a team to rescue him when came a many-voiced shout, "ROCK! ROCK! ROCK!" In the gully above Something was smashing and crashing; under my boots the earth was quaking. Each of us lunged for one side or other of the gully. BOOM, BOOM, BOOM.

All but one were pressed against granite. In the middle of the gully I saw Don turn to this side, find it solid climbers, turn to that side, likewise. I saw him turn to look up at approaching Nemesis, then turn to face the valley and, as if a swimming pool awaited, swandive from the brink. Below a forty-foot wall was a narrow ledge where he'd make his first bounce, then several more walls down which his body would thud-thud-thud.

"MY GOD! MY GOD! MY GOD!"

I thought *I* was screaming. Certainly the scream was in my brain. But my mouth was shut. The scream was up the gully. I recognized it as Ray. I was glad he was screaming. *Someone* should express our grief.

Graceful as a bird Don soared, headfirst. Then in mid-air, he performed a magnificent tuck and roll and was now falling footfirst. He surely was going out in style. He hit the ledge with his feet and crumpled toward the edge. Not quite over. He stood up, smiling sheepishly.

But Ray continued to scream. Not for Don. For himself. In passing, the chunk of granite, big as a stuffed-full Trapper Nelson, had crushed him against granite of the gully side.

I asked Vic and Tom to lead the party to the summit of Garfield, which they did. I led Don (a sprained ankle only) and Ray (in shock from internal injuries but ambulatory) and several followers with undamaged flesh but shattered nerves back down to the road. Their peril was not ended. While pounding a piton for a body-lowering anchor, I broke the hammer handle. The steel head buzzed like bee between the skulls of Don and Ray.

At the road somebody thought to ask, "Say, whatever became of Bill?" I didn't know then, nor want to know now. Presumably, for good or ill, he got un-spreadeagled. I couldn't vouch for it, never having seen him since the rock crashed down the gully. Years later I read an article in a climbing journal by a person with the same name—the same person, I hope.

The reason I didn't give up my masquerade, and the Climbing Course didn't give up on me, was that the fallible leader, though theoretically as self-contradictory as an imperfect God, was unadmitted but accepted. By necessity. Without congenitally fallible false leaders to supplement the few true leaders (who may have occasional bad luck but less often are blundering fools), the school would have to close. I was expected to continue leading and rather than be ostracized, did.

Descending Mt. Constance, to save the time-consuming donning of crampons for a slope of steep, hard snow, I boldly commanded my followers to lie prone in self-arrest position and do controlled bellyflop glissades. One team was unable to follow orders and lost control; the three of them hit a rock, one splattered, and we were the rest of the day hauling a bloody (but living) body off the peak.

Even when not personally present, I influenced events. Scheduled to lead Hibox, I scorned the usual trudge up Box Canyon Creek and the dull scramble to the summit in favor of an elegant high line from Lake Keechelus, traversing Margaret, Rampart, and Alta on the way. At the last minute I was called out of town on business. My substitute led the group of thirty-five along my imaginative route, wrongly thinking that I'd previously taken it and that the trip was reasonable for a weekend. At least the party reached the road in time Monday to call Seattle before the rescue team left town.

I earned a reputation as a leader of interesting climbs. Practice trips, though, were my masterpieces. My students returned from a rock practice up Ingalls Creek, at a new and unscouted site belatedly discovered to be a hell of head-splitting granite garbage, resembling the troops retreating from Bull Run. Weeks after a dynamic-belay practice I had arranged (but was prevented by circumstances from attending), half the student body was still hobbling around on sprained ankles; the serious casualties were limited to one broken leg and three cracked vertebrae. I led a Nisqually Glacier ice practice and we ran out of bandages, one in every four students mutilating his/her calves with crampons.

Snow practices were my specialty. Once, in Commonwealth Basin, a spell of unseasonable May sunshine had caused unusually fast snow which gave exceptionally good self-arrest practice. While exulting in the best sliding I'd ever seen on a practice (and going about yelling, "Faster! Faster! Don't roll into your arrest until you're going *really fast!*), I noted a girl lying at the bottom of the slope at the end of a line of red snow. Rushing to render first aid, I saw blood on her axe spike and a scarlet splash on her pants, plus a hole in the pants, both at a point on the inside of her leg far above the knee. Out of regard for my sensibilities, if not hers, I yielded first-aid duty to a female and got on with my leading. I ascribed the accident to pure awkwardness until blood was flowing all over the basin, five more axe spikes stabbed into five more insides of legs far above the knee, and dozens of bruises and pants holes in the same place. I realized I hadn't warned the students to keep the lower hand at the very end of the axe's shaft; in the high-speed arrests the spikes had pivoted around hands and gone into thighs. None of the wounds was disabling; one lad, though, came within an inch of being unmanned.

On another Commonwealth practice, conditions were more typical for May: a tempest was blowing and the snow was a bog. Only through new heights of bellowing and blaspheming did I expel all 150 students and instructors and groupleaders from tents and snowcaves. When other members of the faculty suggested it was no fit day to wallow in the snow and perhaps the practice should be cut short, I declared this was what practices were for—to give beginners a vivid picture of what sort of sport it was they thought they wanted to take up. I toured the several practice areas, chasing blue-faced students and instructors from shelter of subalpine trees into slashing rain-sleet-snow. I had a paroxysm of rage on finding two instructors and a groupleader building a fire! I grudgingly permitted them to keep it going when a physician explained he'd diagnosed three students as near death from hypothermia.

Shuksan was the end. In the evening I assembled the party of thirty-odd and told them we'd depart at 6 a.m. In the morning I awoke at 5:30 and yelled, "Rising time!" Just once I yelled. After years of yelling I *heard* myself. My loud, ugly voice too grossly violated the serenity of the meadow. I left camp precisely at the advertised time. Alone. After years of harassing people out of bags, on this morning, so calm and free, I said screw it and sauntered slowly up Shuksan by myself, savoring the peace and quiet. Gasping and sweating, they caught up with me at the entry to the Fisher Chimneys and harangued me for shirking my duty. I resumed my role as leader (false leader), a snarling, loud-mouthed bastard, and got them up the peak. But due to the late start, not until next day did I get them off the peak. Personally, I enjoyed the night on the rocks, the stars blazing so brightly and then the light of the rising moon looking so ghostly on cliffs and glaciers. But I wasn't asked to lead any more climbs.

Stick at climbing long enough and one is likely to be dragged into the Great Leadership Debate. It happened to me when we were producing a new textbook for the Climbing Course.

The first draft of the leadership chapter was written by Frank, who saw man as deeply flawed. Individuals he liked and respected. The group, the climbing party, he viewed as a dumb beast that must be kicked and whipped and hollered to the summit.

Franz was offended by Frank's Hitlerism and volunteered to write a second draft. He was a key member of the editorial committee; I had no qualms about welcoming his offer and thought Tom a worrywart when he privately warned, "You know, Franz doesn't *believe* in leaders."

So his draft proved. Franz conceived a climbing party as a commune with one mind and spirit, each decision properly being made by whatever person was at the point at the time it was required. To encourage "leadership" was to profane the freedom of the hills.

No matter our private sympathies; we were preparing a textbook for a school. We asked a third opinion from Dave. Having once been on an expedition where the leader refused to lead, and as a result of climbing the peak essentially singlehanded and having lost his toes and nearly his life, Dave was a convert to leadership. His draft, the final and published one, was a synthesis, saving much of the sweet idealism of Franz, but tempered by the sour realism of Frank.

As for me, I drifted into the third way. Neither a leader nor follower be. Climb alone. Things worked out so well I soon found I no longer had to climb at all. □

MOUNT DICKEY
GALEN ROWELL

"THERE'S NO DOUBT that it was the hardest climb I've ever done; it strikes me in retrospect as just short of phenomenal how well we worked together . . . . Psychically, the thing has really gotten to me; I have dreamed for 15 nights about Dickey . . . . Never has my subconscious been so caught up in a climb afterwards."

I have yet to dream about Mount Dickey. But then Dave Roberts is an expedition cat who has used up many of his nine lives in Alaska. He is also a survivor of the Huntington Jinx, a curse that darkens the history of America's most beautiful mountain. Huntington has been climbed only three times, all by different routes. At least two members of each successful Huntington team have subsequently died accidentally. Seven out of seventeen in all. One of Dave's party died during the descent. Another, Don Jensen, was killed in a freak bicycle accident in Scotland. Dave learned of Don's death minutes before flying to Los Angeles for an American Alpine Club meeting. At the same meeting we spontaneously planned the 5,000-foot rock wall of Mount Dickey for the next summer.

Dave had seen Dickey from a distance during his Huntington expedition. I had actually skied up to the base and touched firm granite — sparkling crystals in pallid quartz monzonite, a granite deficient in the pink feldspar that normally gives warm flesh tones. This technical point would later prove important. Seen from the air, the pink and the pale granite are easily distinguished. McKinley and Huntington are pink; they have perfect rock. The Moose's Tooth is pale; it has some of the worst granite in the world. But I knew Mount Dickey was good; I'd been there and touched it.

I was sure the mile-high southeast face would go if nature gave us the proper breaks. We needed four or five days of clear weather when the wall would be relatively free of snow. This meant June or July and a roulette game with the weather. I had talked about the climb with a group of friends from the West Coast, but as summer neared, each of them declined. By default, our party consisted of Dave, myself, and Ed Ward, a close friend of Dave's with considerable expedition experience.

Dave is right that our ascent went phenomenally well, but only if we compared outlines of plans to outlines of success. On the thirty-second pitch I thought I was further into the jaws of a trap than ever before. I learned an important lesson. I'd always seen truth in the adage, "The only thing to fear is fear itself." But now I realize that confidence can be a more dangerous adversary.

Earlier, I had seen this demonstrated after descending, with three companions, from the south col of the Moose's Tooth. I often wonder if we could have made it by bulldozing ahead with confidence. Many factors had contributed to our decision to quit 600 feet from the summit. We had spent three days with four men in a two-man tent. A 2,500-foot headwall avalanched immediately after we had climbed it early in the morning. We had sat out one storm and saw signs of another moving in. Food and fuel were low. The rock on the upper buttress was the worst granite imaginable—bulging overhangs with the consisttency of Crackerjacks. We had watched in horror as the most inexperienced member of the party nearly lost his boot off the col toward the Buckskin Glacier, 4,000 feet below. No single thing had stopped us. Courage comes from faith, not logic, and our faith had been seriously undermined.

On the fourth day we had descended toward base camp on a glacier where several friends had remained behind and were met by a veteran climber, who asked if we made the summit. When we said no, he stared at us and said in all seriousness, "You chickenshits!"

We had been shocked. We later joked about being "chickenshit but alive," but the event had a deep-seated effect on our psyches. Next time, when trying to resolve a conflict between fear and confidence, we would hear that voice saying, "You chickenshits!"

I had always been proud of my intuition for trouble. Secretly I regarded it as more than intuition. Some kind of ultimate rationality had been bestowed on me. I saw life in counterpoint. I solved problems by hunting for hidden likenesses to things I already understood. I took photographs with the same eye for hidden likenesses, the

Headwall on first day/*Galen Rowell*

dim outline of a meaning or the strong symbolism of a form. In climbing, I tried not to make decisions by rules of right or wrong, which are at best hollow symbols of judgment. I made decisions by immersing my thoughts until either fear or confidence shortcircuited logic.

Early in my climbing days, logic was most often short-circuited by fear. I thought if I could only conquer fear, then I would accomplish wonderful things. I was never seriously hurt. Gradually, over a decade, confidence became dominant. Only occasionally was fear still strong enough to make me retreat.

With hindsight, I can think of numerous friends who must have gone through this same process. Climbing can be a dangerous narcotic. Unsatisfied after the first flush of intoxication, many people become real climbing junkies. In a study of risk-taking athletes, psychology professor Bruce Ogilvie concluded, "They are simply 'stimulus addictive,' that is they have a periodic need for extending themselves to the absolute physical, emotional and intellectual limits . . . of psychic ecstasy found by living on the brink of danger." Studying the effects of drugs, Andrew Weil concluded, "Tolerance is not a phenomenon associated only with drugs. In fact it looks as though human beings become tolerant to any pleasant experience that they indulge in too frequently."

Climbing junkies overdose on confidence. The Greeks called it hubris. Climbers gain confidence in the first place because their basically honest approach works. They discover a feeling of karma—not necessarily as an outside force, but a recirculation of their own actions. It becomes a self-fulfilling prophecy. Faith in one's honesty, confidence, and even immortality is gradually reinforced as climb after climb proves successful. Out of faith comes courage, not logic. And courage divorced from logic becomes hubris, in which arrogance etches away the old honesty. The good vibes of karma silently change into the false understandings of hubris.

The rate of attrition of climbing junkies is fantastic. Many die in the mountains, giving no clues about their terminal mental state. A surprising number stop climbing suddenly and become religious converts to various extreme faiths. Their friends are often surprised when this happens, unaware that their junkie companion has already been a captive of false understanding for years. Some survive relatively intact, destined to move slowly through life like some sort of lobotomized genius, searching through dim recollections of something the brain was once able to do that it will never do again.

I was relieved to find that after twelve straight years of Alaskan expeditions, Dave Roberts is not a climbing junkie. He is strongly motivated by fear, but still possessed with enough confidence to get into serious trouble. Like myself, he has chickened out of serious first ascents in the mountains and had questioning afterthoughts. Once, on a major alpine wall in Canada, Dave forced a companion to give up a direct new route and to traverse off because of avalanche danger. Most textbooks would stand foursquare behind his decision. When one person feels the dangers are too great, the party quits. But Dave wondered about his judgment: "Was he the fanatic, or was I the coward?"

Dave Roberts/*Rowell photo*

Ed Ward is neither a fanatic nor a coward. He is one of those strong, silent types we love in movies and all but ignore in real life. Quiet strength is powerful only in front of a captive audience. Focused on a movie screen, or on a novel page, our attention is forcibly directed to the strange quietness of such a personality. In an actual group, we are most often drawn to people with flair. The comedians and the extroverts get more than their share of the world.

On Mount Dickey, Ed's quiet strength had a captive audience. To this day I don't know how many doubts ran through his mind. I only know that he seemed to make no snap judgments and never mentioned going down. He led quietly and efficiently both on free climbing and direct aid. I felt I was watching a movie in which Gary Cooper was on my side.

Ed Ward/*Rowell photo*

When we went to sleep on our first bivouac, not a cloud was in the sky. A few hours later dawn broke on cloud-locked valleys. White streamers crept up the Ruth Glacier and lapped the base of the mountain. Dave talked about going down; Ed and I were immediately defensive; none of us felt sure about either alternative. We had done more technical climbing on the previous day than on any day in our lives. We were twenty-seven pitches up the wall, nearly 3,000 feet. With five fixed ropes at the bottom, we had climbed for eighteen hours, carrying the lightest loads we had ever taken on a big wall. A tent could not be pitched on the route; so our strategy was to climb fast and light during a break in the weather, rather than haul big loads slowly up the wall into almost certain storms. With twenty-hour Alaskan days, we expected to do the climb in three to five days.

At the bivouac site I outlined the scenario of going down. Rappelling safely meant leaving double anchors each time. If we left fifty nuts and pitons in place, our Alaskan climbing would be finished for the year. Also, we would be descending 3,000 feet through the icing level. If the storm hit, ropes would almost certainly become frozen. We were enveloped in cloud, but occasionally a distant light-show of peaks flashed through the depthless gray murk.

We decided to continue. After several ordinary pitches we suddenly entered an open amphitheater surrounded by high walls of rotten rock. Much of the rock on Dickey had been of excellent quality. We had encountered only one section of really poor rock, and it had been low enough angle not to cause us great problems. Now we were surrounded by rock with the consistency of marbles held together by cheap glue. It resembled overhanging Crackerjacks, like the worst rock on the Moose's Tooth.

The only escape was a doubtful traverse around a headwall on the right skyline. It was Dave's turn to lead. He later wrote this description: "We moved slowly in a blind chillness. I grew paranoid: you could almost get lost up here in the white-out, with 30 previous pitches below. At the top of 31 I was in despair. There was virtually nowhere to go; the rock steepened sharply on all sides, there were no aid cracks, my ledge looked like a dead end. I talked to myself and wasted time searching for an anchor. The impatient call came through the fog: 'Are the ropes fixed?' 'Wait a minute, goddamnit!' I yelled back, knocking in a fifth bad piton."

Soon it was my turn. The only hope was a long traverse. Not to make this pitch would be to admit defeat. Descending in the coming storm seemed impossible. Powered by commitment, I climbed up and out of sight around a corner. A two-inch crack split the face, aiming into an abrupt merger with perfect rock. I placed several nuts for safety, then moved up a short overhang until my hands were jammed in firm rock. At this point, while my feet were still breaking off chunks of rotten crud, I yelled for slack. The rope went up from the belay, then

Nearing the summit/*Rowell*

traversed rough rock and went up again. The rope wouldn't budge. I yelled again and felt the rope actually tighten. In the dull acoustics of the white-out, Dave thought I was yelling "rock" and that perhaps I had fallen. Pinned for long seconds on the overhang, I almost did fall before I finally made myself understood. The crack ended and another traverse brought me to the end of the good rock. As quickly as it had begun, it changed back into glued marbles. Anchor pitons were impossible to place. Bolts would have been equally useless. But thirty feet above me was a tantalizing ledge.

In another situation I might have given up. I was already above good protection, and the rotten rock seemed desperate. But the alternative seemed worse. I convinced myself that I couldn't downclimb the pitch and that thirty feet of sixty-five degree rock *had* to be possible. Up was the only way.

What lay beyond that thirty feet I couldn't guess. It *had* to be better. If not, we were finished. I told myself that the rotten amphitheater was an exception to the rule and around the corner we would find climbable rock.

A few snowflakes sifted through the murk as I took out my alpine hammer. I marveled at its versatility. I had never used it to cut steps in rock. I considered trying crampons, but the rock didn't seem cohesive enough. Pressure on the pick of the hammer dug out a wake of gravel.

I chopped big, crumbly steps—ugly round craters more than a foot in diameter with sloping sides. Each one threatened to roll out my foot as if I were stepping on a bed of ball bearings. Once again I could pull up no slack; so I descended to a rotten stance and began pulling up rope with all my strength. As ten feet came up, I tied it in an open loop in front of me. Soon five cumbersome loops hung from my waist so that I could untie them and provide slack as I moved higher. After ten feet I placed a worthless knifeblade in a crumbling seam. I knew it wouldn't hold but I clipped in anyway. The snowflakes diminished. I was glad, since I imagined that an inch of snow would make traversing the footsteps impossible. As I moved higher the belay seemed worthless and the climb itself futile. I was a child building a sand castle while the tide crept up a beach already isolated from safety.

After an hour of fear and step-cutting I crawled onto the ledge. It was a severely sloping ramp with grooves at either end. I rigged a complex anchor system of poor placements and figured that I could counterbalance the system in an emergency by sliding off the opposite side of the ledge. My triumph in reaching the ledge was short-lived. Above, the wall was vertical and blank. The rock was so crumbly that I hacked out a sitting platform in minutes.

I answered Ed and Dave's questions like a bureaucrat.
"How is it above?"
"Come on up."
"How are your anchors?"
"The ropes are fixed."

Avalanche seen from base camp/*Rowell*

While Ed and Dave jumared up the ropes, I took several runners and leaned around the corner. I saw thick swirls of fog and occasional glimpses of a snow-covered ledge above and to my right. I had no inkling about the quality of the rock, except that it was much steeper than what I had just climbed.

Ed appeared on the ledge with an incongruous smile. I thought he was not really aware of the gravity of our situation. He seemed happy, quiet, and as controlled as ever. I told him that the route lay around the corner, and just after I lowered him out of sight, Dave appeared on the ledge.

Dave spoke freely about our position. The coming storm. The horrible descent. The unclimbable rock. The new rockfall damage to both our lead ropes. I realized later that I put on a facade and answered Dave's questions with smiles and assurance. I suddenly understood why politicians smile.

In his notes of the climb, Dave appraised my calm smiles in the same way I saw Ed's. To him, "the ledge seemed even more hopeless. A blank, crumbly wall loomed into the white-out above. Galen sat at the far end, as gravel trickled between us into the void. 'Where's Ed?' I wanted to say, and 'What now?' Would Galen admit it, that we had run out of choices? Or would he keep that blithe, cheerful countenance to the end?"

People who project false confidence constantly smile when they are being watched. From TV ads, pulpits, governments, and crumbling ledges in Alaska, the results are the same: things that shouldn't happen are accomplished with smiles. Toys are sold to children by showing the smiling faces of other children using them. Religion is dispersed, not from the searching moral centers of individuals, but from smiles of false complacency in a bitter world. The reality of government bears little resemblance to the smiles of a candidate. And on our ledge in Alaska, in a situation in which none of us belonged, two of us smiled while one showed his real fear.

I remember feeling very detached on the ledge. Everything seemed unreal. I felt a scary power that I could hold life at arm's length. It was like watching my own funeral. But I'm not very good at funerals, either. I try to be controlled. To fight normal emotions. But always something unexpected moves me. A tiny thought, a piece of music, the glimpse of a friend, alive.

Maybe the line between sanity and insanity is whether you start screaming the thoughts that everybody has but doesn't admit. Look at Dave. He's probably not half as scared as I am. People think if you don't talk about it, you're not anxious. Dave's done all those big Alaskan routes; so he's probably got more cools than either of us. But the Huntington Jinx. He might be really out of his mind. If we level with each other we'll both start whimpering. I'd better not agree with him or we're doomed.

We overdosed on confidence. Why did we ignore the warnings? The missing pink feldspar. Dave and Ed said the high clouds were often normal during clear spells. And the amphitheater, with its rotten chamber of horrors. Were we too far in to back out now? What if Ed's pitch doesn't go? What then? Rappel? Wait out an Alaskan blizzard? It could last ten days. Shit, I didn't even bring a down jacket. Just a couple of wool sweaters and a ventile parka to save on weight. Maybe McCarthy was right after the Moose's Tooth failure. Maybe the conditions *never* exist in Alaska to get up the giant rock walls. Sheldon says there's eighty feet of snowfall a year and more precipitation in summer than in winter.

This isn't courageous. It's not even fun. It's stupid. I don't want to be here. Hey, all you phony forces out there: I don't believe in you, but I will if you just get me out of here. I'll admit it. Yes, I am a chickenshit. Just get me out of here. Shit, we're higher than El Cap right now, and we've still got 2,000 feet to go. Let me wake up. It's a bad dream. It's got to be. It's one of those miserable anxiety jobs where I've got lead in my bones and I can't get away from anything. Jesus, there are a lot of things I want to do. So much unfinished. It's all happening so slowly. It can't be real. It's not so bad if I close my eyes. Maybe Dave will think I'm resting. . . .

Ed's voice flinched me to attention: "Perfect rock! It goes!"

Less than a minute had passed since I'd lowered him around the overhanging corner. He was back on the same perfect rock I'd touched at the base of the climb a year before. The storm was holding back. It would certainly hit us, but we just might make it to that big ledge only a thousand feet from the top. We could wait it out there if we had to.

This time Dave's voice interrupted: "Congratulations. That was really good routefinding. It might be the crux of the climb. I don't see how you ever figured it would go. It looked hopeless to me."

I turned to Dave and smiled. □

Galen Rowell/*Ed Ward photo*

RESURRECTION
JEFFERY LONG

" 'The chamois hunter go hunt chamois and crystals of rocks, and like his papa and grandsr they are many never come to home ever more. The women pray. They put crucifix, but they are no graves, just wood crucifix. Then sturdy sons go and hunt the chamois and crystal. Then in some years again that family are left without a man. But that hunter have left a son too, and when the boy is stronger he is a hunter too.'

"This was the end of his account. The old peasant was a cripple, and much revered by the remnants of his little family. There are peasants who believe. . .that the glaciers are alive with voices, and that they feed upon lost huntsmen. . . ."

—from the unpublished manuscript, dated 1786, of Michel-Gabriel Paccard's first ascent of Mont Blanc.

AWAKENING, OUR CENTRAL CHARACTER
CONFRONTS TWO POSSIBILITIES. . .AND RETIRES
TO A SHELTER AND FRIENDS.

Beneath a pile of snow Kurtz meadowed, casual, uncold, sleepy in his feathered nap. Kurtz slept awhile, then was called. Someone shook him from sleep, it seemed, an echo almost. Himself it was, calling.

—No, thought Kurtz. —Leave be. This was his sleep, an end without thought, a smug bliss. He gently closed his eyes to doze again. But the filament of snow and sleep was not enough. His name pronounced itself again, and Kurtz awoke.

His mind flushed: What!, and he was immediately raped by a strange and lurid suffocation. He had no desire to breathe. But to move, it was that, that he had to be free.

Against the black stricture of white snow he flailed and squirmed. Responding to his struggle, the snowy socket yielded somewhat. In the grapple his right knee lapsed into its joint and snow worried into his orifices, compelling this blind one to further wildness. His arm suddenly broke through the tangling crust. Air, cold, bit into Kurtz's face. He lay still.

Slowly sight seeped back to his eyes lashed with their ice burns. Kurtz gazed limply through the burst pocket of snow. At once he recognized the place, or thought he did. Eerie colors floated out there, soft and divine. He grimaced in awe of this vision, washed by its quiet radiance. Soft rose cloudlets awaited him, and a serene melody gleamed aloft. Color and song hung like beads of sylphine water. Kurtz lay beneath that world, peering through the hole he'd punched.

—Then truly, he thought. —But no. . .God's lap? For a moment he tried to participate in that bruised vision of grace, then with a quickening realization sank from the holy sight back into this black hole he rested in. —It can't be, he knew.

For a moment he was paralyzed with resignation, sleepy again. But he roused himself. The hole was too tight. His eyes snapped open. All soft colors were gone; something harsher was left out there.

He shoved upward with his free arm and slashed at the snow to escape. The airhole merely collapsed on his face. It pinned his one free arm. Invaginated, crushed once more, Kurtz demanded release.

He strained. He bucked at the torpid snow.

Soon Kurtz rose, alive again.

Not certain why. Not even sure he was. He stood wobbling, a child in some crystal limbo.

He looked at what he saw. Grim fen pillars had congealed all about him, their green ice and purple not like this earth. Kurtz shook powder from himself. Everywhere cold ice. Glass columns issued from the snow and out of the walls and from deeper colonnades. It was a pit of ice. Somehow Kurtz was in it.

—Grisly angels will stalk me, thought Kurtz. —Now the End has come down and I'm trapped alone.

He craned his head back, expecting a mute heaven afire and vengeful with demons. But there was not that, it was something different. There was silence and lifelessness. A lone gray slit in the ceiling far above served to pierce the oubliette. Through it glowed a preterlight, grayness to modulate the brittle green and turquoise ice.

Not heaven, not hell.

—Then where, he wondered.

He walked on. His body was injured, but he felt no pain. Its torn mechanism made him slow and clumsy. It seemed a long walk up the crystal passage, between the walls of the immense chamber.

There was a crude tent ahead. It was a blanket pitched over bricks of snow. When he looked in it he found them. They were clasped, still wringing a final ember warmth from each other, so it seemed. Each was locked in the other's steel arms, immune to the snow they lay upon. There was in their hug to survive no compassion at all, no tender regard for the other.

Kurtz shifted himself, dully watching them doze their brutal sleep. He recognized the one, Adam, but not the other. Still, with snow in their hair, the faces knotted with a last exhaustion. The light dimmed above the world. The world darkened. Kurtz felt weary.

They were too heavy to move. He tugged hard. But they refused to come out. They would not part.

Kurtz weakened. His need to rest was inhumanly urgent. He crawled in.

Old frost rattled down from the sagging tent walls: spent corpse breath. An awful blush filtered through the woolen skin of their crypt. The light waned.

Kurtz shoved meekly against their solid backs and butts and legs. But they were frozen to the earth. They wouldn't move. It was black night washing him to sleep. He slipped with darkness within the darkness.

SOME ODD BUSINESS. THE LAZARUS AND AN ABYSS.

When he woke it was gray day. Kurtz turned his body to see his companion. It was Adam. He stared at Adam's face, at the beard littered with ice, at the gaunt cheeks and retracted slumbering eyes. That he'd had a mode of friendship with this hunter's corpse was possible, but insignificant.

On Adam's far side (Kurtz elbowed up). . .should have reposed that unknown man. But when he looked there was only a shallow indentation in the snow. Adam's circling arms were empty.

Kurtz shimmied from the shelter. Laid out upon the snow mere steps from the tent was the unknown corpse. It was stretched belly down. A lazarus risen? Without humor Kurtz discarded the possibility.

He considered. Had the man been vaguely alive yesterday and perhaps during the night crept out to die? Or maybe, Kurtz allowed, he himself had dragged the corpse out, a somnolent urge. That the man was dead was certain. It did not breathe. It couldn't move. It was rigid.

When Kurtz dragged the body downslope, he noticed one of its arms flapping in monstrous, winding circles. Kurtz dropped the body's feet. Pulling the shirt open, he found the arm had nearly been torn away at the shoulder, perhaps when the man had fallen into this place. Rather than risk the arm tearing off, he buried the lazarus where it was.

And then Adam. Kurtz strained to pull him from the tent, but Adam was cemented there. Kurtz rested. If it was to be buried, he'd need to prize the body from the tent. Tools would be necessary. Kurtz went shuffling, searching for tools. Behind the shelter he found an axe with a thin head and spoon, and thick shaft. Later he found an alpinist's hammer embedded in snow, bluntly snouted and balanced with a long, sharp spur. But by the time of these discoveries, it was growing dark again. As though it were a puppet's power, Kurtz's strength bled away. He stumbled and careened toward the tent. And collapsed into the dark.

Night finished. In resuming the world Kurtz saw he'd not quite reached the shelter. His swoon had caught him outside. He rolled his head. Adam's feet, one of them dangling a wrenched-away crampon, lay by Kurtz's face. Kurtz noted, then disregarded the foot, its iron and straps. He levered himself to standing and with a sweep of his eyes remembered the behemoth chamber in which he was. He would need to explore it.

As he moved downslope, he passed an open hole. It was where he'd buried the dead man yesterday. Now it was empty. Kurtz stopped. He spied the tracks that led away and soon located the lazarus. The body had been pulled toward one of the walls of the chamber. Kurtz noticed only one set of tracks, but dismissed the conclusion. He reburied the body, then moved on.

The chamber composed a rare geography. Its colors were inveterate. They had coalesced through such time and with such fixity that they shimmered a primal global hue all their own. In the dark core of the ice weltered a freezing, incisive rainbow. Everywhere ice merged without certain shape into banks of larger ice.

Kurtz limped between iridescent pillars and walls. His crampons bit and grabbed the snow in ill jerks. The slope slanted down, pitted and rough. He stumbled often. At times the ice thickened and closed above him, and there would be long plates of black walking. Then he'd mildly emerge into the grayness again. The walls narrowed. Soon he was bracing himself against the closening walls, using icy spurs as crutches. Down and down. One knee would not bend but he felt no pain. Curiousity. Not pain.

Two fangs of his left boot were suddenly thrust out into abrupt space. He could go no further. Below him spread an uncertain and huge void. Kurtz couldn't see down into it. It was gray and cold. It fell away, impossibly deep.

For several minutes he watched blankly from his brink. At last he turned to go. The gray light withered. The long day was dying. Kurtz tired. He barely found the shelter. He shoved himself within its glove. Then the night solidified him.

AN ACCOUNT OF THE DAYS.

Kurtz woke. His legs were swollen and heavy. He chose to remain in the shelter all day. He lay motionless beside Adam, who was sleeping. The shelter embraced the occluded space around him. It imparted a sense of momentary sanctuary. Within it Kurtz felt shielded from the sight of the chamber. Its shapes stitched him securely into a coherent or at least intangible world. He passed his eyes up and down the deflated angles, the bowing seams, the walls that were sagging. The roughspun cloth gave texture to his vision. And the heavy muffling cloth gave a reason for the utter silence.

During the day a bed of old snow weighed upon itself. Kurtz heard its slow, temporary slither. Then silence. He listened for other sounds. For the longest time there was nothing.

Nothing.

Then a tiny bell of ice rang. Possibly it had been nicked by a single flake of snow. As the bell's fragile shell disintegrated within its own sound, Kurtz even heard the fragments whisper downwards. Then there was silence. He listened for the sound of himself breathing. Or his heart. But there was silence.

He woke. He woke and slept. Then he woke and slept. It repeated every night, the waking and sleeping. His legs bloated and then shrank. When he could, Kurtz wandered in the chamber, visiting new places. To break the silence and test his ears Kurtz once tried to scream. His throat unleashed no sound though, not even a whisper. A few days later he chopped loose an avalanche just to witness its thunder.

As nights approached, Kurtz took to stretching full out on the snow where he would bid the world its suspension. More and more he slept wherever night caught him. Sometimes he extended his body beneath a serac, or nestled his back against a bluff of snow. It wasn't long before he regarded the shelter as an infection of space. Its walls trapped his sight from the larger hemisphere. The blanket roof was flaccid and thin, an illusion of shelter, no shelter at all. He left it for Adam to sleep in.

Frequently Kurtz passed the various open graves of the lazarus. Every time Kurtz buried it, the lazarus was by next morning uprooted. Kurtz always covered the body with snow when he came across it.

One day he discovered a thread of red color on the snow. He stopped. It was rope worming out of a blunt hole in the floor. Kurtz pulled at the rope and peered down into the hole. It was impossible to see anything. Where did the rope lead down to? Or was it that the rope led out from the hole? He waited for an answer. None came. He moved on.

A MONSTER!

A creature up there. The jackal that was pranking with the graves, Kurtz was sure of it. Somewhere. Kurtz ducked at the thought, then straightened again. He'd known it for a time now. With fast glimpses he ferreted the upper slopes and cavities. Black sockets gaped down at him. They seemed empty at first, but Kurtz began to detect presence up among them. It was a shabby thing, large and illicit. It crouched at the mouth of a slash of ice, watching him. Kurtz pretended not to have seen, then flashed a second glance at it. It was gone.

—Jackal. He hunched his shoulders. Here and there were spoors. Torn flesh stained the snow above camp. Yesterday saw the first of those foul traces. It had come last night too. It had stripped clothing from Adam.

The snow was not simply impressed with footsteps. It was ruptured and torn into wildness. Kurtz followed the track. Perhaps it was the path of this jackal.

Not far distant was a rise of snow-damping sounds. The sounds were timid, their roar cushioned by the muffling snow. When Kurtz reached the top of the rise, he caught sight of it. It was a man, ridiculous with bulk. It was wearing Adam's jacket outside of its own, and three or four pairs of trousers.

It was flinging itself against a tower of ice. After some minutes of this effort, it would roll in the snow or gape its mouth open as if to yell. No sound came forth. Closing, then throwing its maw open, the jackal twisted to and fro. Kurtz stared. He felt no shock or loathing. Simply wonder. He watched while the corpse closed its shattered mouth upon its already shredded forearm and tore a strip of flesh away. This was chewed but not swallowed. Because it was dead. It could not swallow. The masticated flesh was dropped from its loppy mouth. When the jackal began tossing its rigid hands over its head, Kurtz walked away back down the trail.

KURTZ IS MORTAL BUT COLD.

He was without heat.

Beneath Kurtz's bare palm the snow and ice never melted. He grasped sticks of hanging ice and pressed his open hand against milky pools of glass, but the print of his touch was always unrecorded. Even a lone snowflake stood immutable on his wrist. One day he slashed a groove into the ice. When he returned, after circuiting the chamber for weeks, maybe more, the groove was nearly absorbed back into its bed of ice. Kurtz regarded this, then forgot about it. He was trapped in this eternity. The trails he made sank slowly down into smooth snow and vanished. The nicks his axe made evaporated. The chamber and its walls were shifting organically. Kurtz noted this huge convulsing beast, but he had no place to retreat.

KURTZ IS IMMORTAL BUT DEAD.

With cursory fumbles Kurtz managed to pull his coat and shirt partially off. He examined himself. His flesh was turning a vague, mottled green. When he watched his vitreous torso for the rhythm of breath, he found nothing. Kurtz realized he was dead. Or seemed so. He pawed the shirt and coat back onto his shoulders again.

Fascinated by his cadaver, he shoved at his pants until they bunched at his knees. He stared at his penis. With an effort he passed a thick, brief stream of black urine that soiled the snow.

—My soul, mused Kurtz.

KURTZ AT THE CIRCUS.

When he sighted the jackal far ahead in a smooth crater, Kurtz stopped. It was lurching stiffly through the deep snow. Then it slowed into an idiot's posture and fell over, arms waving and gangly, legs gently pumping as if it was still walking and not lying sprawled in the snow. The jackal twitched like this for awhile, then recovered and walked on. Kurtz knew, as he watched stock still, that those were his own motions too. It was the dull gravity dragging him into physical stupor at each proper thought, and it was each thought forgotten while he directed himself toward a physical place.

As Kurtz stared after the jackal, it suddenly halted and flogged the air with its arms. Then it disappeared. Kurtz followed its trail, curious, but stopped just short of an oblong hole. The jackal had fallen into a crevasse. It was gone.

There was Adam the man. Kurtz unearthed him from the collapsing shelter. Adam was asleep as he properly should have been, mostly naked now because the jackal had taken his clothes. From his puddle of dreams a line surfaced to mark Adam's purple lips. Kurtz decided it might be a smile. Adam's arms still banded an empty circle.

His legs and all the joints of his body swelled and withered, then swelled again, then withered. Kurtz began to count large sections of time that way, marking months with the wax and wane of his tissues. When they were swollen and thick, Kurtz often lay still for entire days. After the tissues had drained again, his limbs would crack and snap with each step. If he was careless his right leg would unjoint. He never felt any pain though.

KURTZ FIRST THIRSTS FOR THE GRAIL.

It was during one of those days when his legs were swollen and Kurtz couldn't walk that he discovered the hope. Upon first struggling from the shelter where he'd spent the last nights, he saw it. It was the lazarus climbing the headwall of ice. It was miles distant, the headwall, but that black mote suspended near its base was without doubt the lazarus. It was climbing out of the chamber in obvious flight. Kurtz collapsed in the snow, his legs too bloated to walk.

The lazarus made no progress that day. It didn't move. Kurtz ignored the figure for hours, then tried to trace a slight alteration in its position. There was none. It was stationary throughout the day. Next morning Kurtz detected a slight progression. That same afternoon he poked his head from the apse of the shelter, scrutinizing the lazarus. It was motionless, no higher than in the morning. Next morning showed the lazarus had crept still higher on the headwall.

—So it moves only at night, and while I sleep it escapes, he realized. —Why. Why while I sleep. And why flight. Why such energy, he wondered. —And why not. Through the day Kurtz drifted, thinking. He broached ideals and counter-ideals, then scoured their words. Finally he conceived a point to ward away plain thought. For no other reason than that it seemed reasonable, Kurtz left that very morning, hobbling away from dull, pink Adam, chubby in his ever-sleep.

CONTEMPLATION IN SUSPENSUS, KURTZ EFFECTS ESCAPE.

Kurtz mounted a long series of plastic ripples, slow in his movements, retarded by his body that was tattered and green without pain. He gripped the smoke-rusted axe and with a touch reset the snugly belted hammer. His crampons chewed at the floor, stabilizing the earth.

High overhead the lazarus hung without motion. Kurtz glanced up at it on sudden occasions, trying to catch it moving. But the dark spot was always still. The lazarus had atrophied on the glass wall and become an exhausted dalliance staid by the force of day as Kurtz was by the force of night.

When the headwall interrupted his plod, Kurtz paused. The wall was sheer and glabrous. Its opaque spectrum wattled the wall, black to whited ice, so that it seemed to Kurtz he stood at the center of a brilliant, colorful star. The colors rippled like glass muscle. He laid a numb palm to the surface. His presence made the ambiguous ice firm, and a sort of clarity wavered into focus. The maze of watery runnels fused.

With dull, unbrooding power Kurtz smashed his axe into the mass. The ice was brittle. It flaked away, shedding his axe. He slammed its spur into ice again. This time it teethed behind the skin. He kicked. The claws purchased. His leathern foot lifted from the ground to retouch the dimly burnished ice. And he moved again, increased his height. He postured in balance and struck the ice repeatedly.

The dancer moved. Each step and strike was an explosion. Tiny portions of the wall slivered. Chips leapt like gray sparks. His thick calves jumped, locked, and unbunched. The ice flowed before him, squeaking with every metallic kick, fracturing into slight fibrillating nets around his toe points. From the axe head sprang brattled spider webs.

When the ice bulged in a viscous impasse, Kurtz sculpted his way over it. He broke glass steps into the wall, steadied himself with the hammer. In a long throat of delicate razoring tissue he shattered his way through, daggering higher.

Upon reaching a brief shelf, Kurtz looked around. The chamber floor was far below. Effortlessly he continued. Higher he stopped again. From this height he could see hundreds of crevasses lacing the flat floor. They twisted and wound through neighboring slashes, their coiled rifts tangled like latticed branches.

—And are there crevasses bellying the bellies of those crevasses?, Kurtz asked himself. For one uncontrolled instant Kurtz froze, caught in a gulf between action and thought, paralyzed by nothing. . .by a premonition, maybe a memory.

But he unholstered the hammer and swung it again. Tapping his front points once more in continuation, lifting, he danced absolutely fearless on glass.

Kurtz stepped and struck, stepped and struck. There was no monotony to his motion. Nor was there any frenzy. He was a calm man reaching forward. The gray daylight blackened. His inertia flagged. He found another shelf. He locked his limbs, quit himself into sleep.

HE IS INTRIGUED WITH THE GRANDER METAPHYSIK.

The blighted colony set soundlessly beneath him. It was a dot. Inside the dot that was a shelter that was a blanket was Adam, the man. Adam slept, smiled, dreamed within a dot. A dot. Kurtz didn't giggle or murmur, snicker or sigh. He couldn't. He stared at the dot.

There were no sounds above him. The lazarus was still and hung like a swag of force. It was driving up and out. But for all its nocturnal energies, the lazarus above was merely a dot like the dot below.

For a moment Kurtz sensed his game. He was now suspended between motes. When he reached one dot, the world would still be the world, but the dot would not be a dot. It would be a world. Once abandoned, that world would sink back into its dot. Relentlessly carrying World from dot to dot, Kurtz unfroze with the dawn. He recovered and drifted higher, floating upon his mechanics.

He spun away from the chamber and its reliquiae, away from the jackal, the red rope trailing from the hole, the blanket-shelter, Adam and Adamic sleep. He rose on.

A RELIGIOUS SENSATION NEAR MID-JOURNEY.

His fingers played rapidly over the smooth bulge. There were no holds, no friction to stick him to the wall. Without his metal tools Kurtz could not have raised this expedition towards the lazarus, the gray slit, and flight.

He needled higher, points licking in and out of the ice. One day, near blackening dusk, Kurtz had still not found a shelf to couch his inert body through the night. He perched helplessly upon his tools, searching higher, and sensed dark weakness stealing through him. His naked fingers scuttled furiously across the ice. But discovered nothing. He balanced, unbreathing. With no ledge to hold him in the dark, he would fall.

As the light filtered away, his grip visibly loosened on the shaft of the axe. His muscles flickered tender spasms, more fluid and weaker each moment. He decided. It was the only way. With a flash of motion he slammed the long, sharp spur of his hammer through the wrist of his opposite hand, fixing it to the ice. He stared at the impaled limb. He felt his feet drop away, one, two. He hung there noiselessly. He felt his body sway. Then darkness ate his eyes.

He woke to his crucified hand. He awaited further gray light to feed him back to strength. He recovered his feet. He jimmied the blade from the ice and his wrist. There was no blood. Kurtz continued higher.

KURTZ ACHIEVES HIS IMPETUS AND TOUCHES IT.

The beast that was the icewall coiled and slid away; Kurtz obeyed its postures. Almost without knowing it, he glided closer to the lazarus.

On the ice there were no landmarks to notify his position. Each moment of the ice was without an absolute feature. Maybe deep inside of the ice lay the echoes of a geologic personality, but on the skin of the wall there was simply ice.

Nevertheless, there was passage. His metal fingers pricked into the crystal, retracted, dipped sharply again. On shelves and steps Kurtz occasionally paused, remembering he could walk as well as clamber, stand as well as dance. Near evenings he would reflect on flesh, on ice, and on sleep. He watched his flesh blemish with sores of ice. His joints faltered, but he climbed. Every day he climbed a little more. Then slept.

He pulled up and over the step. There was a booted foot planted heavily on the ice. Frosted eyelets, laces and wraps were thick with verglas. The boot's metal teeth held its sole off the ice. Kurtz traced the boot to leg and higher. He saw the towering, dormant figure.

He touched its boot, grabbed the woolen thigh, pulled its belt, and gripped the shoulders. He'd caught the lazarus.

KURTZ BECOMES FIRST PARTY TO A VISION!

He'd caught it. Now he could surpass it. If the lazarus escaped, so would Kurtz. Where it went, Kurtz would be before. He glanced upwards to the gray slit, the exit, the further world. Soon, soon now. He would escape this chamber.

As he clutched the immortal shoulder, Kurtz caught sight of his own hand. The bare fingers were white and tinged with verdigris. It was a deadman's claw, Kurtz knew. He could almost smell its souring color.

For a moment the lazarus vanished. In its place stood Kurtz, propped against the ice. Alone, immobile, Kurtz roamed an onerous trance, a future. With time the ice would yield behind him, he saw, enclose and encase him. He saw himself swallowed indifferently. Time, maybe more than centuries, elapsed in his vision. During thaw would come his release. Wet with the melt, rigid he would be, limbs knitted with age. Sun, then a wind fresh like lime, would come and lick him. His soft skin would dry, corrode, its powder join the wind. The skull a whistle, then even the bones to soft dust. Kurtz saw Kurtz become the wind. He watched constellations he'd never seen curl and unbend patiently, dimming, flickering into lifelessness. His dust would come to settle when the wind curdled. And with the last star's last glister, he would even in flight have reached not anyplace.

Kurtz closed his eyes. He felt blackness crushing him, but had no desire to break it. When he finally looked again, he was lying against the wall of ice. The lazarus was beside him. Its congested eyes stared straight ahead toward the gray slit of beyond. The lines of determination in its mask were a grimace now. The lazarus was driven. It would rise out of here. That much was printed on its face. Kurtz sensed its truth. . .a quiver toward the starless night. The lazarus was an animal of the ice now. It moved in contradistinction to the ice, implanting a line of ascent on the formless medium, a line already shifted, a thought already lost. In escape, as in a word or a drop of blood, there was purpose. But purpose for the sake of purpose?

A SOMEWHAT DASHING ARRIVAL.

In the day Kurtz climbed. In the night climbed the lazarus.

Each morning Kurtz came awake at the first gray light. The lazarus would be lying beside him, having moved up in the night. During the day he would climb high above the lazarus, then stop at darkness. Next morning the body would be nearby. Day's creature was joined by night's. It was soon difficult to discern which was ascendant, the day or the night. Kurtz accepted this.

The gray slit widened above him. It became a whale's mouth gaping open to the sky.

After the trial of days spent climbing and nights without dream, Kurtz crawled one afternoon through the lips of the ceiling, out from the ice chamber.

As he bunched his legs under him to stand up, Kurtz collected thanksgiving for his terminus on the outer earth. But he found himself in a vaster chamber.

At first he believed he was on a mountainside enclosed by clouds beneath a summit and flat sky. But it was a chamber just the same. There was ice here as in the place from which he'd come, also without wind and sun.

The gray slit through which he'd crawled was merely a crevasse in the deep belly of another. High overhead Kurtz located a thin, gray line. That would be the hole towards flight, the mouth of yet another crevasse, to yet another chamber.

Night came. Kurtz slept.

The lazarus arrived that night.

In the morning Kurtz found its tracks in the snow. The trail led to one of the faraway walls.

A CATALOGUE OF EVENTS.

On his first day in the new and larger chamber Kurtz ambled. Before the night came on, Kurtz came across the lazarus splayed on a bank of snow. He pulled it to an ice cave. He buried it with snow.

Of course it was gone next morning, risen, as was its habit every night. Kurtz spent the vacant day searching but couldn't find the lazarus. Near dark he was back again at the burial cave. He pitched himself down just as night struck.

In the morning Kurtz woke to find himself covered with loose snow. Someone had stuffed him into the ice cave's pit. It took him nearly half the morning to extract himself from the grave. A clumsy line of steps marked the lazarus' path. It had visited.

He followed the thick stream of ruptured snow. The body was still. The lazarus had flopped and dragged this far before day had overtaken it. Kurtz bent and shoved at the body. It flipped onto its back. Was the face more determined? He passed his eyes downwards.

The lazarus' sleeve was empty. No hand filled its end. The arm was not there. Kurtz hunted for the missing part.

It spoiled the purity, the blank spread of snow. It was the arm. It was naked, a device unjointed from the body at the shoulder. The arm had finally fallen off. Kurtz burried it separately.

The next morning the arm was not there. Its little tomb was empty. Kurtz searched for the arm. He kicked the snow. He stabbed here and there with his ice axe but failed to turn it up. The lazarus was gone from its larger tomb. Maybe the lazarus had taken the limb with it.

In turning from the ruined graveyard, he spied something. It was the limb, obscene and bloodless, clinging to the wall. It was almost within Kurtz's reach. It was absolutely still, but by its tensed muscles it seemed ready to shiver into action. The fingers had bitten around a handle of ice. From the tattered dags of shoulder flesh to the tips of its fingers, the arm was an ill green. Kurtz waited for the arm to bend or the fingers to regrip the ice. But it clung stiffly dormant.

He considered dislodging the handle it was gripping. By touching the limb Kurtz thought to goad some sort of action from it. Instead he simply watched.

He traced the cracks and ice bubbles by which it had risen to its place, then postulated the remainder of its path. Sooner or later it might escape from the chamber. The lazarus was disintegrating in its hope.

Kurtz looked at the trail the lazarus had left.

—And is that the final term of resurrection, wondered Kurtz. —To always be in flight? And is that the pattern? Trudging off, perforating a blank field of snow?

Kurtz faltered. He fell. He lay still. He was caught in an odd bubble, the victim of a tedious metaphor.

He knew without exploring that there would be a brink at one end of this chamber, over which he would not dare to go. He knew that the gray slit high overhead would not be the last gray slit overhead. He knew there were probably other jackals in this and other chambers, hunters who'd quit the ascent that contained a purpose that contained itself, who would devour themselves in a semblance of passion. He knew the lazarus would escape again.

Kurtz's fingers were turgid with the cold. The straps of his crampons were glazed solid. They wouldn't come undone.

He wished to rid himself of the tools, to toss away the hammer and the axe. He felt he should drop them down a hole. They occupied his hands seductively. But they could take him...where? They were useless symbols.

And yet Kurtz couldn't release the equipment. There was the chance he'd misunderstood something. He cradled the tools. He would wait.

Kurtz touched a pocket of ice.

He stiffly settled into the cavity. He was wasted and gaunt. Ice hung from his hair. His legs seemed not to be his anymore. They were folded oddly and grew like roots into the ice floor. He tried to burrow deeper, to curl further. Time passed.

From somewhere crystals of snow began pattering down onto his body. Perhaps it was the lazarus brushing burial snow onto him once again. Kurtz gazed without concern while the cave filled.

Finally he found himself staring through a small hole. At last even the hole began to fill. Somewhere a spine of snow released slough-offs. Distant ice flutings tinkled in answer. His eyes closed.

They opened. He was captured in tight darkness.

With violence he tried to breathe the darkness, but would not breathe. His fingers stopped their motion entirely.

And at that, at last, he almost smiled, not grim, not pleased in this myth he was. □

SPRING WEEKEND LOVE AFFAIR
ERIC SANFORD

FRIDAY AFTERNOON. Cramp four. Smell of creased knickers; tinkle of aluminum money. You can feel a hastiness in the air. What am I doing here? What are THEY doing here?

Berserk repetitive strokes up the burning, stone-cold vertical highway. Fill 'er up and check my water. Thanks. A ten-cent tip and you're on your way. Village spamburgers; A5 traffic.

Just finished a twenty-hour bivy in the snow after four off-route pitches. Four days is just too much—gotta come down. Froze my ASS off! Think I'll become an armchair mountaineer, a real boon to my sport. Hell, if you don't climb, you can't hurt the rock. Everybody but Royal hurts it anyway. Why try?

What a great bunch of routes. Dotted lines and rest areas. A tram to the top of the Apron? BHOS Dome? Coonyard. Magic Mushroom. Bet Royal's pissed! Where's Batso now that we need him? Think I'll sneak a route up the back side of Half Dumb: *"Up Yours. VII, 5.2, A6.* This highly unaesthetic cynical climb starts two hundred feet to the right of the left-most dihedral just before a giant spider web located three hundred inches directly uphill from a large tree. Unenjoyable, dirty climbing then leads to the summit. This horrible route, having been climbed once, will hopefully fade into well-deserved obscurity. Carry hooks, of course. Bashies useful. . . ."

Talk drifts toward my van window. . .incessant chatter by prophetic janglers—hard 5.6. . .had to come down. . . dropped a jumar. . .it's pronounced "u-mar". . .see this new rope. . .WOW. What is THAT? . . .AHHHHHHH! Shut up! I'm trying to hibernate. Back to my *Ascent*. Let's see. . .5.10F. . .Where's my *Mad*?

OK, move all those campsites back a hundred yards. WHAT??? A blueorangeredgreenyellowbrownprimusmolybdinummacaroniropeghetto. Who stuffed toilet paper in the sink? Wish all those damn groads would move over to Yellow Pine. "Why don't you take your twenty-four-hour-a-day jam sessions, your groady dogs, AND your 'hoots,' and SCRAM!"

Back to the van. Let's talk about being bummed out. OK. I'm bummed out. Probably leave. . .last time here. What's it all about, anyway. What is climbing in Yosemite Valley, U.S.A. all about?

Well, it's about IT, and it's about US. WE are the flat-footed coeducated blue suede semi-local 5.10 hopeful hot-dogs. IT'S. . . .well, what can you say. It is Yosemite. Too bad it and us can't get together to write the laws. Section 4.3, Article 8: Anyone caught using a piton takes a forty-foot leader fall. Second offense, your belay anchors pull. There's no third time. . . .

So now it's chalk marring the rock, ruining the "natural wilderness experience" for the next guy. What I want to know is this: just what "wilderness experience" am I ruining? You mean to tell me that people actually come here expecting a wilderness experience? You think anyone actually wants it?

Yosemite is no longer any type of wilderness experience. New York is. Miami Beach is. Los Angeles is. Yosemite is not. It is simply a one-by-five-mile vertical gymnasium with car-campers in the bleachers. Period. Sunnyside locker room. Leaning Tower trapeze. Half Dome Bar and Grill. Twenty-two water bubblers and an audience. Score: one to one. You lose. Don't get me wrong! Heavens no! I love it here. . .for what it is. Came here four years ago. . .learned the ropes. Free showers, ice, food, laundry, TV, movies. . .shhhh!. . .don't tell anyone. And tomorrow another first-timer: steel 'biners, greenline, new set of polyhydrofleximatic nuts. Shit, gotta sell all my old ones again. Never even used them. And to him it will be just like it was to me four years ago. If you don't know what to expect, then whatever turns up is OK. On the ground, that is.

Just part of the SouthFaceoftheColumnpinnedout Blues, I guess. Yup. "Supplied with four topos, two guides, seventeen gallons of prune juice, twelve pounds of bologna, ninety-five pins, one hundred and seventy-five nuts (kept at the bottom of the haul bag; 'ya, we took more nuts than pins. . .'), eight ropes, bashies and mashies and smashies and trashies, bolts (thunder), three *Masked Marvel* comic books, and a spare pair of BVD's, we trudgened ever onward." Oh, no! We forgot the ice axes. Any of you guys seen an ice axe around? I've got a modified custom-chrome twin-shafted duplex Brontosaurus. Funny, I knew something was wrong. Had to come down. . .after the crux and all. I thought the crux was leaving the ground? No? Climbed up one pitch, rapped off two. Did some interesting caving. Got "bummed out" by all the fixed pins. What? Ya, had to leave a couple to rap off, you know. A1. A nested rurp#10hexjumarbashietie-offcanopener. Must have pulled. Found it in the bushes next to a rusty sardine can. . . . Just part of the blues.

Made some new friends. Good ones. Much talk. Wish I had some Winnebago stock. Nasal off-key blues pierce the air. Ukulele Larry is at it again. Wish the "mad bolter" would take care of *him!* Think I'll spend next summer on the Oasis. With my luck they'd start the Firefall again.

Think I'll get ready for a climbtapebenzoinchalkcontactcementepoxyEBkneepadwhitesuit. Let's go. North Buttress of the Chin-Up Bar Direct. Maybe after, the Parallel Bar, Left Side. First free ascent, 1980, by Morton Monkey, on loan from the LA Zoo. Think I'll name my new route the Direct Direct Direct on the Direct Direct. I climbed it by rappelling upside down. Should have brought my TV. Why not be comfortable? Isn't that what it's all about?

Perhaps comfort is just one of the things which have combined to ruin Yosemite Valley. That and automobiles, fire, horses, potato chips, Curry Company, communists, vibram, and people. Least of all climbers. How can someone who sleeps like a bat and smells of that from which he came ruin anything? Climbers are simply like everyone else: they take advantage of the ruination. Sunnyside my ass! Where IS the trail to Yosemite Falls?

Let's all go somewhere else. Tuolumne...the Tetons...Wind Rivers...Alaska...Patagonia.... Hell, let's all go to the North Pole! Man is certainly no different than any other animal. He just plays his part. The dinosaurs once ruled the earth (or so we are told) only to become extinct by over-using and under-replenishing their environment. And the dodo bird, gone too. And now man must look forward toward his future and his possible extinction. When will "progress" end? Can I live in Site 23 forever?

So now the incumbent climbers must look to the future with introspective eyes and decide if they should fill igneous voids with only nuts, thus limiting their aerial progress, or form their own voids and fill them with bolts; both are so much a part of the technological era which Reinhold Messner despises, yet one carries a bit more risk than the other. But from a purely ethical standpoint perhaps some magical, undisclosed number of nuts constitutes the same rucksack-stuffing courage-load as a ten-pound bag of bolts and an electric drill sharpener. Who will draw the line?

Really! How artificial is a bolt? A guidebook is a bolt. You find a climb that interests you. Get some inside info. How hard? How long? Who did it last? When? Approach? Deproach? What do I need? Pin list. Topo. Off we go to seek our death-defying wilderness experience natural adventure. Now the clincher: it was ruined as a natural experience because there was chalk on some of the holds. Shit! You're lucky you didn't have to stand in line. Real lucky! Try doing El Cap in May. Six parties a day. Hurry, they'll catch us. Hurry, they won't. Don't worry, to hell with 'em. ROOOOOCK!! A can of peaches whistles by my head, earthbound.

Had to nail the headwall in the dark. Slept in slings all night. Ten feet from the ledge; couldn't see it...didn't know it was there. Dropped my glasses. Dropped the haul bag cover. Dropped the haul bag. It wasn't so bad. Big walls are a walk-up. Lotta work. Dirty. Lucky parties hit a storm, have some adventure. Forgot my ice axe. Where

IS my ice axe? Too hot. Too cold. What if you can't come down? REEEEEEEEESCUE! Natural dangers (climbing being one of them). Read the latest AAJ. How many accidents are actually attributed to something other than human error?

Yosemite Valley is man-made. Climbing is purely a technical problem. Did you do it all nuts? All free? No rope? No hands? Who is our guiding light, Hot Henry or Joe Sunday over on the Apron having an epic? EB stands for EveryBody. And after all this, how come EveryBody has joined in the cry for ecological climbing? "Oh well, you see. . .I've been telling people for years. . .I've been saying all along. . . ." Face it: Yosemite (pronounced yō-sĕm-īt) cannot be saved. Not from me for you, or from you for me. Does it need to be saved? Does it need to be saved just for climbers? Why? If you are following a pre-scribed route, someone else's creation, how can that be any more of an adventure than copying someone else's painting? Is a Winnebago the same as a covered wagon?

Why chop a bolt because *you* didn't need it? Perfectly good nut crack right beside it. A #7 wedge in at a twenty-seven-degree angle. Bomber. Falling! Ahhhh. . .pop! Ahhhh. . .I'd just as soon be safe. There is low-risk poker, after all. There are low-tar cigarettes. Should there be low-risk climbing? The book says 5.7, A1, but it goes free at 5.10M. What the hell's wrong with doing it 5.7 A1? Nothing. Protection, ratings, chalk. . .they're all part of the game. Who cares? Isn't climbing doing your own thing?

Came down off that damned thing. That guidebook is incredibly confusing. . .shitty route description. . .got lost twelve times. . .had to leave a sling. . .my best one. Was it Moses or Batso who said, "I don't give a rat's ass what anyone says about my route." Really! God bless the holy guidebook! Chapter XIV from the book of Roper; Arch Rock. . .funny how that little green book can have such effects on people. Maybe the next author can ask first ascenders from now on whether they want "their" route "ruined" by subsequent ascents or not. If they don't well, ". . .this unpopular, devious, dangerous, rotten, unprotected route is not recommended. . . ." Funny, I thought it was A1 when I did it. Rather fun, you know.

The Yosemite days make me think of the dawning of man. The Valley fills me with such happiness and elation in revealing all its splendors to us lowly creatures. I'm so surprised that Sentinel hasn't crumbled at the obscenities we, yes, you and I, have written upon this once-virgin valley floor. Is the view from Glacier Point real? Is the sight from the Wawona Tunnel to be believed? We are all in heaven already and don't even know it. We must all pause and let our minds capture the magnificence set before us. Surely this must last?

Sunday afternoon crazyfatmommarideoutoftheparknoisymotorcyclecamperslipstreamvolkswagenagogo. Whee! They're gone. No more day-glo sneakers and golden pitons strung on peeling necks. Back to the hardcores. Bums. Dirty. Think I'll do a climb. Anybody seen my hammer? □

BALTORO
PHOTOS BY JACK TURNER

Back from Baltoro:
wild roses in bloom
at Paiju—the name
means salt in Balti,
but no salt here,
just dust, dirt & rock:
narrow gully choked
with scrubby trees
where porters sleep,
Baltistani hobos' jungle,
empty now: smoky
firepits, small black stones
round which Baltis bake
their hollow bread, Tok.
But now, coming back,
we don't even stop,
pass Paiju & its roses,
put it out of sight
past riverbend, all this:
glacier's gritty snout,
canine teeth of unkind peaks,
month of madness, hurts
inflicted & received by all,
all of us, for nothing:
climbs not worth climbing,
film not worth filming,
endless demeaning fights
with porters, with each other:
clashes, standoffs, silence. . .
Put it behind, pass on
down valley toward Askole,
no backglance, no regret—
down there wild roses
blooming thicker still,
Braldo river running
muddier still & deeper,
too deep to cross direct
so detour now for miles
to high hanging bridge
of broken twigs & vines
swaying cliff to cliff
across from Mango Gusor—

(Mango Gusor, snow thumb:
rock spear!) Magic names:
Masherbrum, Trango,
Mustagh & Gasherbrum,
Broad Peak aflame
in duskfire, Baltoro sunsets
& moonmilk nights
staring up at chalk towers
from Urdukas' grass benches.
Too much, too many names
to save now, say again:
Lilego, Korophong, Bardumal—
waterworn rocks, pebbles,
sandshelved canyon floors,
abandonned camps, illusions:
expedition's end, bareboned
wreckage of ill-laid plans,
winding down, going home. . .
& what to take, bring back,
salvage from this cold
Karakoram countryside?
A glacier season gone,
only wild roses to bring
back from Baltoro.

Lito Tejada-Flores

Page 70: Paiju Peak and the Trango massif from Urdukas

Page 71, top: Porters preparing a meal at a rest stop

Page 71, bottom: Bridge over the Biaho River

Pages 72-73: Looking up the Baltoro Glacier from Paiju

Page 74: The fabled Mustagh Tower from just above Goro camp

Page 75: The great north face of Masherbrum

SMILEY'S INITIATION
DAN BURGETTE

Smiley is a farmer. That pretty well describes him. Shoveling grain has built up his right arm enough to chin himself a couple of times with it. This feat won him admiration and envy among the climbers in the Purdue Outing Club because none of them could do that trick. By the time he was a senior, Smiley was a farmer who did some rock climbing.

When plans were started for the P.O.C.'s Third Annual Cold-Fingered Hibernal Assault of the Nation's Biggest Tetons, Smiley decided to try his sport in the real setting. So it happened that he was one of the six Hoosiers that dug a snow cave below the Middle Teton in late December. The weather was good, and on the thirty-first Smiley bashed steps up the South Teton with three others. He had passed from a rockclimber to a mountain climber.

After his success on the South, Smiley was hot to do another. And this time he wanted to learn to use crampons. The glacier route on the Middle is easy enough in the summer, so Smiley and I set out to initiate him to ice climbing. It was 9:00 a.m.

Avalanches had swept most of the glacier clean, and polished ice gleamed at us invitingly. Smiley attached his crampons on the lower glacier and began scratching his way up the brittle surface like a geriatric crab. As we approached the crevasses of the upper bowl, we started wading through thigh-deep snow. We could not find any solid snow beneath our feet close to the largest crevasse, so we set up a belay on a large ice block. I put on the rope and did an end sweep around the crevasse, and cut back just under the next one. When I reached a patch of bare ice, I socked in a hog and front-pointed over the upper wall. Just above, I put in two screws and belayed Smiley.

I led and Smiley followed. The sky was blue, and the ice nice, as we continued onward. So did the clock.

The upper neck of the glacier was an enjoyable mixture of black ice, snow, and snow-ice. Depending on where the rope ran out, we belayed from screws sitting in stacks of brittle ice chips manufactured by the screw, screws driven into porous ice that reminded me of Rye-Krisp, or solid wart hogs in black ice. The latter wasn't the rule, sad to say, but Smiley didn't seem to worry. When the angle eased up toward fifty degrees, I decided that maybe this wasn't exactly a beginner's ice climb. But Smiley followed every pitch without saying much. Didn't know enough to worry, I guess. Mainly he was just glad that we didn't have to go down that way.

At the col, Smiley shared his jelly beans and gum drops with me. We realized that we were moving slower than we had hoped; only an hour and a half of daylight remained. We figured that we could make it to the summit by dark and descend the southwest couloir easier than we could rappel from screws stuck in Rye-Krisp—besides, it would be cheaper. Up we went.

Right away the ice was replaced by snow. It was unconsolidated and our crampons scraped on the rocks beneath. After one hundred and fifty feet, I belayed from "that time honored symbol of security," an ice axe driven into the snow as deep as the rock permitted it to go—since it was a short axe, it was almost to the head. Smiley wallowed and scraped on through to a rock a hundred feet above. He anchored himself to his axe and I joined him.

After half-heartedly stepping onto the seventy-five degree snow plastered against the rock and hearing it settle a bit, I followed Smiley's urgings and tried climbing the rock. When I was ten feet above him, my points ran out of buckets, my fingers were freezing, and I retreated downward. Since the rock decided that I was a better snow climber, I gingerly traversed around the rock. The angle relented and I swam upward. A rope-length above, I could see the first real crack we'd seen all day. The fifteen feet below it was extremely steep snow. To make matters worse, the top six inches was almost consolidated while underneath was a bottomless sugar bowl. Burrowing up through the last ten feet was like climbing an overhanging sand dune in an icebox. Eventually I slipped a nut in the crack and belayed Smiley.

Time was flying. The lowering sun was turning the first clouds we'd seen in days a lovely orange. Too bad they were storm clouds. Time to hurry. The gully is a scramble in the summer, but now every foot had to be worked out.

Hurry! Up the steep snow again. Dig a trough and swim up through it to a small overhang. Clear snow away. Thread a sling around a chockstone. Stem up, traverse left. Pound an angle in a rotten little hole. Drop a mitten. Freeze your fingers probing for more holds. Getting dark. Smiley wants to know if we should go down. Too late; no flashlight. Get another mitten out of the pack. Probe some more. Starting to snow. A wide stem; the axe goes into a crack. Pull on it like a jack handle and up you go. Jab the hands into the snow and push. We're over it. Smiley comes up. "Wha'd ja do here?" "Just do it!" "Tension!"

It's nearly dark as he comes up the snowy gully looking like Patey's ghost. He leads through to the crux chockstone, one pitch from the summit. I follow and it's dark.

My first impulse is to keep going. Smiley wants to bivy in the cave beneath the chockstone. Decisions. Decisions. We can't see, it's snowing, we've no light, and the cave is fairly large. But: it's fourteen hours to morning, it's January 1, we're not prepared to bivy, we don't know how bad the weather will be by morning, and if we can get to the summit we can probably get down OK.

Smiley is all for the bivy and I'm rather beat. I doubt if I can lead the chockstone blind. We'll stay.

We tried to stack things in the corners where we could find them in the morning. Smiley explained that a person is only a farmer out of desperation and predicted that he'd make out here, too. He took the shovel, and we started to wall up the open side of the cave. The crust made fair blocks, but the sugar beneath was useless. The blocks ran out before the wall was done, but it was better than it might have been. We sat on our packs and Smiley sat on the rope. We had an extra down parka for our legs and we loosened our boots. Fifteen minutes gone and 825 to go.

Smiley's initiation into ice climbing was about to include his first bivouac—mine, too. Our feet soon cooled and we wiggled our toes mightily. We told stories, laughed, moaned and sang songs—most satirically morbid. Smiley was stoic about the cold. Hardly said a word.

Every so often I would ask if he were still awake, just to make sure. I didn't try to be a stoic. I moaned and whimpered, being naturally loud and obnoxious. Someone had to keep us awake.

The storm wasn't too bad. Rather warm, even. Spindrift sometimes got in to us, but we held our own. Sometime in the morning the storm moved off and the temperature dropped. The moonlight mocked our misery and made it seem like it was always just before daybreak. The snow we were leaning on melted and soaked our shoulders to the skin. Our breath froze into an icy sheet a half inch thick over our parkas; spindrift covered everything.

Sometime before dawn, I dozed off to sleep—just a few minutes, but enough to lose the feeling in my feet. They felt like chunks of wood in my boots. No amount of wiggling would warm them. Smiley never nodded off and his feet were cold but mobile.

The shivers had my body in their grasp by the time the sun finally rose. Smiley wasn't too bad off and I was impressed. He was psyched up to lead us out of there, so I made the motions of belaying him. There was an old pin in the left wall of the chimney and a sling around a chock higher up. He couldn't quite reach the pin so I took the lead.

I grubbed the snow from a crack with my axe, and threw a nut and a sling into it. I stood on the sling and rummaged through the snow and chockstones until I found a hold. Then I stemmed onto the old pin and clipped into the sling above. Some big jugs helped me swing from under the chock, and I reached the snow above. The snow was good, and I soon reached the notch above. After much hassle hauling the pack, Smiley emerged over the crux.

From the notch I figured it would be a snap. It wasn't. We were weak and winded, and all of the rock's secrets were hidden by loose snow. I tried twice and fell once. Smiley tried twice before he succeeded in getting to the snow above and on to the summit above. Then it was my turn to get some tension as I joined Smiley. Three and a half hours had been consumed reaching the summit from our bivy cave.

The day was brilliant and the snowy peaks all around were truly beautiful. We were too tired to take pictures, except with our mental cameras, as we descended the southwest couloir.

Friends met us at the saddle and took my pack. Smiley was still chugging along. We got back to the cave, ate a bite, and skied out. Smiley reached the valley at 10:30 p.m. after a rather long day. We ate steak dinners before I went to the hospital for my frosted toes. Smiley survived his initiation all right.

Smiley is back on his flatland farm now. He says that next time he goes ice climbing, he's taking his down booties! ☐

Lo que el alpinista tendrá presente

Todos los ejercicios tienen sus reglas, cuyo cumplimiento interesa a todos aquellos que los practican. El alpinismo también las tiene, y de un interés tal, que su incumplimiento puede acarrear graves contratiempos.

El alpinismo se propaga rápidamente por todos los países, que han comprendido al fin el enorme beneficio que de los ejercicios realizados en las montañas se pueden obtener para la salud. Etimológicamente, alpinismo significa deporte cuyo objeto es efectuar excursiones por los Alpes; pero se hace extensivo a las excursiones por las montañas en general.

El entusiasmo por estas excursiones data del año 1741, en que los turistas ingleses Windlhan y Pacocke exploraron el pintoresco Valle de Chamonix.

Hasta hace poco se ha creído que el alpinismo era un ejercicio fatigoso sin beneficio alguno físico o moral, siendo lo contrario, pues practicado con moderación y haciendo preceder las grandes ascensiones de otras preparatorias, lejos de sentirse fatiga, domina al excursionista una sensación de bienestar.

Aparte de esto, cuando el alpinista llega a la cumbre, se siente satisfecho al contemplar la belleza con que la naturaleza se rodea en las alturas de las grandes montañas, donde la vegetación cesa y sólo se contempla hielo por todas partes; las glaciares, con su acumulación de nieves, no tienen nada de la naturaleza de abajo, y el alpinista se cree transportado a un mundo nuevo, desolado y muerto, pero de una inmensa belleza.

En España la afición por estos ejercicios va aumentando de un modo ostensible, y día llegará en que esté desarrollada del mismo modo que en los países cuyo aliciente principal de turismo lo constituyen los deportes de invierno.

En nuestro país existen multitud de sitios admirables donde el alpinista puede saturarse de belleza al encontrar los enormes desfiladeros, las altas cimas, la osamenta inacabable de las montañas, los parajes desconocidos, los dilatados horizontes, el manchón de árboles que se recortan allá en la lejanía.

Un equipo especial es indispensable para el alpinista. El vestido ha de ser ligero y caliente a la vez, debiéndose desechar todos los abrigos que estorben los movimientos. La camisa de franela es necesaria, y el traje interior completo de punto de lana, muy conveniente.

Las señoras también son entusiastas de este deporte, y el equipo femenino requiere también atención. Las enaguas se reemplazarán por unos pantalones abrochados por debajo de las rodillas y las faldas, que serán cortas; por medio de botones deberán poderse levantar algo para que no impidan la marcha en las ascensiones difíciles. Llevarán un cuerpo o blusa de tela forrado de franela, con cuello ancho; el sombrero será de fieltro.

Además, un saco de grandes dimensiones (fig. I) que se adapte bien al cuerpo. El calzado será holgado y fuerte, y los accesorios más importantes para la montaña, como el bastón-pico, no le faltarán jamás. Sobre la nieve el alpinista debe pensar en proteger su cara del sol; no deben aceptarse, para este efecto, las pomadas que dan un tinte verdoso, sino la máscara negra (figuras II y III). La elección de cuerda tiene tanta importancia, que por mucho que se aconseje sobre ello no se da un concepto de ella. Una buena cuerda debe reunir condiciones que parecen contradictorias: solidez, ligereza, flexibilidad. La seda es la substancia que mejor reune esas tres condiciones. Al mismo tiempo que el alpinista aprende a colocársela (figs. IV y V), debe aprender también a plegarla; el trenzado en cadeneta (fig. VI) tiene la ventaja de poder desenvolver la cuerda en un momento.

Para aquellos alpinistas que llevan un guía los crampones ofrecen muchos defectos, pero para los que caminan sin él, que deben hacer el rastro por sí mismos, son unos auxiliares inapreciables; en la nieve dura evitan todo trabajo de talla y son en el hielo una gran seguridad. Los crampones preferidos no tienen nada más que una articulación (fig. VII) y se ajustan por medio de espesas correas (fig. VIII). Sobre los glaciares, donde el alpinista debe proteger sus ojos con las gafas amarillas; los peligros de los precipicios le amenazan, pero la cuerda arrollada al pico (fig. IX) suprimirá este peligro. A veces, obstáculos temibles se presentan y es necesario proceder con cautela, y por una maniobra, a menudo larga y siempre delicada, nos esforzaremos en arrojar la cuerda por encima de cualquier espesura (figs. X, XI, XII). Entonces, a fuerza de puños, los dedos crispados alrededor de la cuerda, el alpinista salvará el obstáculo. Los lazos para pasar la punta del pie disminuyen el esfuerzo a realizar (fig. XIII). Para bajar precisa también observarse las reglas siguientes: Después de haber puesto la cuerda sobre un bloque saliente rodearemos nuestra pierna con ella (fig. XIV), luego los hombros (fig. XV), y el descenso comenzará (fig. XVI). Con un poco de esfuerzo y buena voluntad lograremos que, a poco, nuestro pie toque en el suelo y nosotros nos encontremos en seguridad, después de haber contemplado durante largo rato las galas de la Naturaleza y descansado de los afanes del trabajo cotidiano.

JANUS
BOB GODFREY
PHOTOS BY AUTHOR AND DUDLEY CHELTON

"FREE CLIMBING...." Two simple, easy words conjuring up images of graceful ascents.... flowing movement... Zen on the rock face... keep John Muir in mind ... don't hurt a rock. "Free climbing...." Two simple, easy words... bedeviled by discussion, paradox, and conflict.

"Free" is the Janus of modern rockclimbing. Aspirations toward simplicity and purity of style exist in the context of intense debate, and sometimes intrigue, surrounding new ascents. It is a paradoxical situation:

> ... he wears almost everywhere two faces; and you have scarce begun to admire the one, ere you despise the other.
> —John Dryden

Those who free climb at the highest standards seeking maximum purity often find themselves most immersed in public debate of the subtle complexities which frequently accompany new routes. Simplicity is a goal...complexity is the route by which it is reached. Free climbing doesn't hurt the rock...but sometimes traumatizes the psyche. Paradox after paradox.

The early pioneers, or their ghosts, must chuckle. The rocks were once a no-holds-barred arena of frolicking delights in which a piton, or a bolt, left no soul-staining mark; only a dent in the rock. Today, the puritan concepts of sin and guilt are deeply embedded. The insertion of a piton wreaks more havoc on the conscience of its inserter than damage to the rock face.

Shrive me Father....
For I have sinned....

It is all too easy for the modern climber to downplay the achievements of the pioneers. The historical ego-trip is satisfying, and who remains to question? Yet a modern free ascent is in no absolute way "better" than an early ascent which used direct aid. Layton Kor's ascents in Colorado of the Wisdom Roof, the Diving Board, and the Naked Edge, using direct aid, were breathtaking feats for that period. So many factors were unknown, equipment was relatively crude, and technique was rudimentary. Today, the climber arrives at the rock with the best of modern equipment, shoes with glue-like frictional properties, chalk, and a guidebook which maps out a climb and gives a precise description of its technical difficulty. The style of Kor, in Colorado, in the sixties, was absolutely appropriate to that period of time.

Free climbing a route which previously depended on direct aid, using clean-climbing techniques, is very appropriate to the 1970s. Times have changed, attitudes toward climbing are different, and styles which were suitable for one decade are not appropriate for another. The question, "better or worse," is simply the wrong question to ask.

Free climbing has its own particular joys and satisfactions, not the least of which is to back off rather than hammer iron. But the apparent simplicity of free climbing is confounded by contemporary events, by debate of issues, by questions of morality, and by conflicts between freedom and social control.

The concerns are real...undeniably. Classic climbs deteriorate and the hordes continue to multiply. The biting edge of competition is never far below the surface... and the ego-less state is a myth.

Death and Transfiguration

A return to styles of the past, shades of the back-to-nature romanticism of Rousseau, where nostalgia obscures reality, solves nothing. The Puritans undoubtedly led chaste lives, but blandness is one of the by-products of overly zealous morality. The application of puritan principles to rockclimbing homogenizes and colorfulness is lost. The stultifying effects of feelings of sin, guilt, and psychic anguish over right and wrong can inhibit a climber's energies as much as the pull of gravity, or the fantasy of hitting the ground. Modern preachers, with their, "Thou shall. . .," and their, "Thou shall not. . .," of pious concern don't help.

"Forgive me Father . . . for I have sinned,"

"I used aid without telling."

"I chipped a tiny hold."

"I placed protection from a rappel."

"I did willfully covet my brother's climb."

"I did lust to see my name in the guidebook."

"Your sins are unforgivable, my son. Thou shalt writhe in anguish in eternal damnation."

Free climbing is here, and is probably here to stay. For reasons of aesthetics and environmental concern, more and more climbers will likely choose to climb using free methods. The great debates will die down. Preachers will go out of business and simple free ascents will take place in a loose, easygoing atmosphere, reminiscent of decades past.

Free climbing . . . . . Two simple, easy words . . . liquid patterns . . . experience simplified . . . time and space redefined . . . existence revitalized . . . poetry . . . joy . . . and the simple beauty of supple movement.

The accompanying photographs show modern free climbing in Colorado. The climbs depicted are among the most technically difficult modern free climbs. Because of the acknowledged lack of precision and logic of the decimal rating system, and the debate which accompanies its application to the more difficult recent climbs, ratings are not given.

The photographs form part of a series which traces the development of Colorado rockclimbing from the late 1800s through to the present day. They are to be published in book form in the spring of 1977. The book has been two years in preparation. Approximately 100 classic Colorado rock climbs have been photographed by means of extensive rappelling and jumaring to reach the best vantage points. Additionally, many previously unpublished photographs are included which depict historical rock climbs from 1919 through to the present. The text of the book is rich in anecdotes and details of the adventures, foibles, and follies of those individuals who have made the greatest contributions to Colorado rockclimbing over the years. □

Vertigo—Direct Finish

THE AEOLIAN WALL
LARRY HAMILTON

At noon Friday I am alone with my dog Fred, in a white car speeding south and west toward Las Vegas. The desert unrolls in its endless red boredom; the speakers blast out the same tape I've had on since Vail. Discomfort is dull, constant, and irrelevant. There is one purpose: to get there and Do It. The car is hot; the dog drools in silence.

THE TOP of the face was gone and the sky was black with clouds. March winds were gusting down-canyon in our faces as we picked our way across to the approach gully. Four hours to get up it, Herbst had guessed. I hadn't believed him; it looked so much shorter than that. We were both wrong.

Before long the hiking ended, and we took out the ropes as cliff bands broke our gully. There were loose traverses and off-width cracks, long chimneys and steep brush as we slowly gained height. The hauling was always desperate. It was mid-afternoon before we finally had a clear enough view to realize that our approach was completely off route.

The bushes grasp and tear, scratch and threaten to blind. Cactus jabs treacherously from below. Strength and spirit ebb, drained by the uphill struggle (I am not used to this) against gravity and harsh vegetables. The face frowns down, distant and aloof, watching us crawl. We're nowhere near it yet.

With much cursing we descended into a more useful gully and proceeded up it to the last headwall below the bench under the face. It looked sadly impractical. Herbst set off at once on an imaginative line of holds, but they and he stopped some forty feet up. Unwilling to just downclimb, he balanced there painfully and drilled for a back-off bolt. Snow fell gently, piling up on all the unused holds. The omens, I thought, seemed to be getting insistent. Why were we so sure? In this evil weather?

But the snowing ended and Herbst came down (in terror of his hasty bolt), and we descended once more to try a different tack. He had spotted some steep cracks to the right which he thought might go at 5.10. I wanted nothing to do with those and set off, despite his warnings, up another deceptive face. After a crumbling, mossy, ill-protected rope-length (and what seemed a very long time later), this last major obstacle of the approach was below us. It was nearly dark and the face loomed huge above.

With the fall of night the sky cleared and the wind died down. We built a fire and made cheese-and-salami sandwiches as the cheerful confidence of our synergetic personality seeped warmly back between us. We stared up into the shadow and tried to guess whose pitch that great, hulking roof would be. The bivouac was made miserable by our inspired expedient of bringing only one half-bag, to share.

All photos by author

TOWARD DAWN the wind rose again and we were grateful for the sun. Herbst snatched the first lead (having concluded, I think, that the roof would be on the fourth) and after some nice crack climbing (which he made look easy) plus a few yards of aid (which he made look hard) arrived at a chimney-bottom belay. I led through gingerly, up the flared and blocky chimney and on up the long aid cracks above it. I was running out of everything—another of our weight-saving, time-wasting expedients. And so it went. We were following a spectacular dihedral that ended four hundred feet up at the disturbing roof, which crossed half the face and seemed to block the sky.

A climb's best moments are often its rests. It is there, retrospectively, that the last pitch seems so fine (though you couldn't wait to end it, at the time); that the view becomes ultimate and one's thoughts expand.

I hang from two pins in a horizontal crack, secure as Herbst hollers and fiddles above. I don't know what he's doing, but I do know he'll get up it; he always does. I photograph lichen. To the left the wall curves out darkening, from red to shadowed gray-green. Here and there damp chimneys and rubbled ledges emphasize the bald desert blankness. My right horizon is the dihedral wall I lean against; it's much too big to peer around. I can only imagine what the yellower face out there looks like. I've been here before, perhaps in a dream.

I have a deep distaste for desert flakes, stemming mainly from a more general fear of death, but given special sharpness by an incident which befell us three years before on Aeolian's magnificent sister, the Rainbow. We had limped down from that wall with a smashed haul bag (goose down spraying to the winds), a trisected rope, and an indelible warning scare.

So now, on the Aeolian, the hollow section of the roof was bolted, no questions asked. The rest went on blades, and I continued for a while up the confusing face above, to belay standing on a bong in a squeeze chimney. It was getting late, so it was up to Herbst to find a ledge (I was sure there was one there—it had held snow that winter) at the end of his next lead.

"How is it, Joe?"

Mumble mumble. If it was no good, we were in trouble. As yet another expedient, we'd left behind our hammocks and belay seats.

"It's OK to jumar," he eventually yelled down. "I think the anchors are all right, but don't get too rowdy!"

What an ugly thing to say, I thought glumly, as I jumared to his palace. Crotch Ledge, as we affectionately came to know it, was a triangular hole four feet on a side and filled with rocks and snow.

"Ratshit!" cried Herbst, for the fiftieth time that day, as we surveyed our dismal bed. Another wretched night. We munched more incredibly delicious cheese-and-salami sandwiches and talked. About our wives, whom we missed, and about the progress of our very different lives. There is a darkness in his past, from a time before I knew him (and I still know little) that contributes a shade of ambiguity to his light and open present. Camp 4 blind dates, we came to know each other on a five-day El Cap epic. We'd gotten along and had continued to climb together once a year or so since. I counted with fingers: this was our eighteenth shared big-wall bivouac. It was certainly one of the worst.

ABOVE THE LEDGE the route was entirely free. Herbst scuffled up through an overhang in the early light. Beyond it he puffed and complained a bit ("This is long! It looks like Midterm!") and threw down a lot of moss, but he continued to move up the crack (which did not look at all like Midterm) with smooth competence. It eventually opened onto a slab where, after placing our eighth and last bolt, he belayed. As I led on up the exposed, slick slab (Do you see? I'm not falling off! It *can* be done in Robbins'), he was making some thoughtful and abstract comparisons of our "heads" for climbing, differing panic reactions, etc. My pitch ended in a cave, the most comfortable place on the climb.

"You're tied off—but don't be rowdy!" I called down cheerfully, then retreated from his expressions of dismay to go back and sit on the anchor.

We were accustomed by now to chill, windswept belays and to the fact that the sun left the wall at eleven. But our third day took us deep into the cold stone itself. Above Crotch Ledge, the upper half of the face was carved by a single, water-worn chimney system which arced directly toward the summit. We were thankful for the bland skies; this would be a grim place to be trapped by wet weather.

We were glad, too, for every ounce we'd been able to leave out of the bags. Hauling was awful. The second man was continually forced to jumar on the outside of the flared chimney, wearing one pack and pulling the other up

hand over hand behind him. And although the leads were free, they were seldom easy. Our progress was slow.

My watch stopped at twenty to five yesterday, but it feels about lunchtime. I rummage in my pockets for another filthy lemondrop and redistribute my weight on the crackling belay bush. No ledge, just a bush. We are tied off to several of its thickest parts and to one good nut as well, but it all seems insubstantial. No matter. Things are going well enough; we'll be off tonight, and I feel no alarm in noting the high, thin clouds that forewarn of what is to be the West's worst storm of the year.

There is no sweeping vista, no roaring exposure now. We are in a vertical canyon, looking out at a broad stripe of bright world. Herbst has vanished around a corner in search of a new line. He is very dubious about my assurances that it was the way to go. I'm glad it's his lead. I wonder if he feels the same relief about mine, or merely humors me, thinking he could do them faster.

I'm hungry and tired and cold.

Late that afternoon we finally topped out, weary but unable to relax; it would be a long way down. As the sun set, we encountered a lost hiker, who fell in with our hurried descent. When a rappel was necessary, we lowered him. We tried to impress upon him, gently, the folly of his ways and the gravity of their consequences, but probably just confused him. Where did we learn all these tricks? (He wanted them too.) He told us that he had a friend who had climbed with pitons and things in Yosemite and who had assured him that this sandstone stuff was worthless.

But we knew what had happened to the good stuff in the Valley and what was already encroaching here (we had brought it ourselves). Two weeks before, one of America's foremost first ascensionists had attacked with pitons and siege tactics a long, free route which we had flashed clean, with Tom Kaufman, on a cold day earlier that winter. We'd felt a hopeless and silly outrage at this intrusion of insensitive outsiders into "our" area. The Golden Age of the Red Rocks had surely passed. Joe Herbst, author of nearly all the area's hundred-odd routes, was taking up tennis. He would shake his head sadly and explain to me once again why this had to be his last climb.

We ate a late dinner in Vegas. It was a time for glowing and gluttony; the calm before the storm in which all our reasons seemed so clear. We could barely stay awake.

At noon Tuesday the same white car (smelling of dog) and I (and the faithful mutt himself) are speeding north and east. The same Al Stewart tape is blaring in our ears. We are to meet Leslie at seven in Grand Junction, still four hundred miles away. It's raining like hell and one wiper blade just flew off, but everything else seems fine. I'm looking forward to spending the rest of our brief vacation exploring trails and arches with my wife and sitting beside her on flat rocks in the sun. □

BROOKS RANGE
INUKSHUK
KENNETH ANDRASKO

"GARBANZOS!! Garrbannzzohohohos!!" Come on out, furry critter, if you're there; let's dance and act brave and then run away from each other right now if it's going to happen. Let's get it out in the open, not suffer fright and mutual cardiac arrest in the dwarf-willow gully with boulders—my, they look pretty solid, almost granitic, though shy on the hornblende and mica and too flinty. Maybe there *is* good rock back in the Divide as hypothesized; these must have washed down from back there; can't see through, though. "Garbanzohoho!" Well, here goes, into the thickets, at ease, fully at ease, right? There are no bears, of course, but can't seem to forget that *News-Miner* headline last week: "Grizzly Bear Eats Photographer." Good old *Ursus horribilis*.

Been traveling through this valley for a week and no big critters seen yet except for those Dall ewes up a side valley, hinting at the good possibilities back toward the Divide. But still hesitant; too many gnawed caribou antlers and nights alone on the tundra. No other movement. Wading the Sagavanirktok River three times at night to enter the valley was numbing—"Swift Water" in Nunamiut; the name is appropriate. Just after a two-hour flight from Bettles, landed here in a spot forty miles from the one chosen, but at least there was motion.

Stripped naked. Lying out in the sun all day; yeah, wilderness is the ability to maintain an illusion of virginity and fresh gales of innocence, or something like that.

Looking for animals again, always. But the pipeline-archeologist job was pretty good that way, sitting in a meter-square tundra garden that's reduced from Persian carpet lushness down to a Japanese stone and sand garden in six inches, after a full day of troweling. And all the time watching for eagles and gulls and all of those red and arctic foxes and the wolves. And the one wolf chased late at night out into the endless quagmire, the two of us doing a dance together after he came up to the open tent door: first me after him, freezing whenever he turned to watch, him thinking I'm a caribou (after successfully getting up-sun from him and prancing well). Out-of-breath loping through rice-paddy tundra, camera held high as he chases me at last and squints into the horizoning sun and finally kneeling to await him, steady, letting him come as close as he will before he finds no antlers (ah, good photos). He's elegant in eventual disinterest; I'm exhausted and drenched and clear-eyed wading back to camp, but we've danced together tonight, he and I.

THE CARIBOU should be running south. It's mid-September and ice forms on stagnant ponds and only me running with my packs, ferrying loads of beans and gas and my one ice screw for the north faces that should be steep and glaciated. What if there really *is* ice in here, somewhere among these peaks with delicately etched white couloir systems, photographic negatives of Ipiutak ivory carvings, of whaler's scrimshaw.

It's all a bit silly, walking through here pretending those graceful antlers aren't outstretched hands grasping for my stride with jagged jealously. The whole valley is a graveyard by bygone motion; a depository for antlers and skeletons lost in transit. Why don't the caribou run south through the pass like they're supposed to? Where are the ones that run now and don't reach out to drag me under into their permafrozen graves? I came to be with the ones that run free and canterlope.

This nameless valley itself is an antler, with so many years gone by—count the streams running into it; each is a point indicating a season. All the side valleys are branches of the main one; antlers in their own right, venerable ones with lots of couloir points. I'm an Eskimo hunter right now, spotting and counting and peering through high mists at grunting gullies slithering in alto-cirrusian reverie: braided and bouldered torrents crossed by Dall sheep, oracles of ice to come. Antlers and skeletons comprise the reigning visual alphabet here, itinerant forms reassembled in the mountains high above in all possible scales: pale glacier tongues look like shoulder blades, gendarmed ridges like toothed jawbones, and lichen bits like twelve-point racks.

Boulders are spread out on the stream's broad fan like a game of *wei-che* (Go, that is) gradually maneuvered into strong clusters and pathetic solitary forays by meltwater torrents. Hey, that looks like bare ice up this gorge. The stream's stones are near-granite; it's worth a reconnaissance tomorrow. The stream drones on into another stanza; a

Gregorian chant but a little more ethereal, like that all-Eskimo band in the Chena Bar on honky-tonk Second Avenue in Fairbanks; it's a droning yet polyphonic drifting-snow sound.

An amazing gorge, so tight and neat with spires above. Ah, a snowy ptarmigan there, in awkward flight. I'll follow her and try for a photograph. Just up this next hill, though it's out of the way. Almost; damn, in flight again; just chalk scattered against a slate sky. Following the ptarmigan mother's decoys allows me to pass a major cul-de-sac; she actually led me the way toward that peak which mimics the ptarmigan's browns and whites. I'll call it "Mother Ptarmigan Peak." The route is the perfectly natural and correct one; I'm guided along it without decisions.

On every ridge giant boulders; Ipiutak Eskimo carvings ten feet tall slowly rotate to follow my movements. Immobile, yet ever watchful in their stony silence. Nanuk, the polar bear, in conglomerate, standing upright just ahead, like the one I saw at Ripley's Believe It or Not in Atlantic City as a kid; jeez it was huge. Ah, seal! It splashes to the left in the boulders. A chess set of carved figures but alive and without set spaces or rules for motion: *ugzunakpak*, the giant shrew panting there; *tinmiagpak*, the stone ptarmigan again, popping up first in periphery and avoidable, then right *here*. A crisp white apparition arrives instantly ahead, slender curves of motion incarnate: an antler in grotesque poise.

I'm gambling in a casino without knowledge of the rules. It operates by itself in silent mockery, a wilderness of possibility and contained, articulated fear that spurs and commands precise action always. There can be no slips on the steep iciness that lies ahead. Flowing cautiously up that moraine should give a view around that corner...my god! another peak there! and bare glaciers plunging straight downward, incredibly beauteous—have to call it *Samvega* peak, Sanscrit for "aesthetic shock", as I recall.

Ever since that first day in the valley when I found the archeological *Inukshuk*, the "stone men" cairns set up as decoys to block entrance to the valley and scare the running caribou into waiting lances, the valley's been alive, saturated with the spirit and world of the Nunamiut hunters once here. Each of those slabs of stone tells a tale to other hunters who know their secrets, warning of daemonic *iuqiqiq* and *atatiq* ghosts or locating good fishing spots—perhaps they were, like the northwest winds, harbingers of storms to come. Or maybe they told of the delights to be discovered in this hidden cirque. . . .

FINALLY, moving with only a rucksack and hardware—one screw for the icy faces. Hello, another sheep skull, sinewed eyesocket intact, second one today. Have they simply lived their days, or do they fall from above?

Crampons feel fine, first time since March in New Hampshire. Only thirty-five degrees here above the glacier, but it's perfect bare ice with the faintest touch of powder. Solo means complete commitment, surety, and faith. Getting pretty steep now after a couple or three pitches; it's hard to measure and divide a climb without the rope. Better abandon French technique now and go to front-pointing. Ah, that feels more secure. But wait, it's got to be done correctly, it's all for me alone now, so let purity prevail. Yes, push the beauty of French rhythm until the limit is surely reached. The Brooks Range is a wilderness, an area where the maxim of life "beyond a reasonable doubt" is null and void; doubt abounds, so fascination must balance fear. There is a fantastic array of potential and possibility in these virgin peaks; their questions far outweigh the answers, which have little value here. Ignorance looms large and is important, for wilderness is an indulgence in a controlled folly—being on the verge of momentous revelation, living just this side of fear in a system whose logic is not understood, exposed to its ravishes and caprice.

Ah, my Chouinard axe and hammer take their toll, swiftly and gainfully employed to whisk up another four hundred feet to the couloir's crest, all front-pointing now on fifty to sixty degree ice. Close to a thousand vertical feet climbed with only a break for photography to record the vast valleys of ochre and amber, these burnt colors of late fall. The gully top at last, fine view of Ptarmigan Mother's 1,800-foot north face, challenging; maybe have a look at it tomorrow; for now, a photo of us both, rig up the self-timer.

The summit: call it "Dancing Antler Peak." Now, traverse that knife-edge to try Samvega; surmount these gendarmes with delicate and—my goodness—hard fifth-class moves; descend to that gorgeous thousand-foot stream of ice that flies right to the summit, rising from the glacier and valley that once were across the Divide, its hitherto unseen fierce couloirs and delicious streams now shimmering like beaten gold.

An unstable cramponing spot for sure, quite exposed. This wilderness challenges the completeness of the world I see by offering elements undreamt before. Yet I'm climbing, eventually, in a place where actions have no

consequence because they are right and true. The carefully placed ice axe strikes home every time, no second swings despite the hardness of the ice. It seems there is no possibility of falling when each crampon, axe, or hammer point individually arrives firmly and intact, as if its course and trajectory have been carefully calculated, as if they are only acting out some well-conceived plan.

Samvega's summit rolls gently down sheep-tracked slopes to the south, belying all its other steepnesses. But I've vowed to climb only the most direct north face routes, or none at all.

LUCKY THING old Ptarmigan Mother's lower ice patches weren't bad—I've got to start hiking out tomorrow. Hey, some of these granitic handholds and flakes have edges familiar from a former association. Let's see, must have been the east face of Garnick's Needle in the Wind Rivers; yeah, that was quite a few years back but hasn't changed a bit, same old firm handshake, no doubt about it. Others bear uncanny resemblance to ones I knew high on the north ridge of the Grand in a steep corner that seemed pretty desperate at the time, with Andy ill all the way, feeling for holds—yes, these are the ones, same truck-driving fit, rough and untanned. Howdy, good to see you again.

Lots more are almost look-alikes. Like when I'm off traveling and keep seeing—well, almost, guess not—the faces of friends in the crowd, now portaged by unfamiliar bodies. Wander the valleys like Fellini does the streets of Rome, studying the faces for ones that strike or entice, then engage them for the next project. Never forget that Aleut cleaning lady in Fairbanks, her face grimed with centuries of oppression, poignant and so thoroughly in the present, unapproachable, unavoidable, and dear.

The gully. Its sides stand firmly in refutation of the low angle the basaltic gully bed offers; they're not even geologic kin—where the steepness swoops it's that near-granite again. The gully is an intruder, injected into the rent of a family quarrel ages ago. It welcomes another stranger now, beckoning: come and see, come *here* and dance lightly. Looks okay, but the way really did seem to be to the left. Might as well have a look-see at this pale gully, a bit slippery with fresh powder, uncertain and confusing in its paleozoic code, probably more recent than the dark granite. It *should* go. Well, dude, this is getting a bit much, skidding in lugged treads on a fine film of powder, sensitive to neither light nor touch, not a silver glaze responsive and warm, but a cold blackness in those icy stares. Hard to read, this sparse calligraphy of Altaic or Akkadian, alluring and like some cascading extract of cream, but where to place fingers and feet from here? Intuition's blind and momentum mute, hands reaching for cracks that aren't there, soles gripped but not gripping, childishly hanging from a frozen overhang for minutes already, fingers stiffening into wooden clothes-pins clamping the hardened thorax of a giant cicada who's molted

and miles away; the frozen skin parka of a careless Eskimo boy pulled from the bergy waters, hanging on the line drying in the cold swift breeze; it's *all* on the line now.

Shaking, finally made the move, *get something in!*, gingerly, wow, this is for real, got to find the token hardware slung on that sash across my chest, a diplomat's Orders of Valor or general's insignias of rank. Ah, yes, my confusion affirmed by grasping the line from a high nut. Hold on! with the conviction of a lad with his first kite in a high wind, barely able to remain on the ground. My god, it would be very foolish and final to fall from here, I'm hang-gliding from a cracked nut, I'm not deciphering the route's stone hieroglyphics at all. I mean, sure, a little rusty and no hard rock work for months and all, but this is serious stuff, man, you've got to get warmed up to the idea. There *is* that rope in the pack and three soft pins for retreat, but courage, old boy, steady she goes and all that.

That's it, gently, reverse the move; it's nice to see those nuts in. Something isn't right, just slow down and look things over a minute. Yep, the steep buttress holds the key, sure; only two moves confirm it. Back to the well-known granitic system of folds and seams; slowly advance up a circuitry of spaces and voids; avoid the forms surrounding the cracks and suspended in defiance of Newton, floating idly by virtue of an exquisite electromagnetism.

This buttress is swift in its self-appraisal, so proud and true. Well, let's see, perhaps a twelve-league-booted stride to bridge that gap and stem the tide of indecision. Dear Yvon, thanks so much for those tiny Stoppers, ah, the frenzied dancing they allow! But there's no silent signaling to another in the neo-Inca knot-language climbers choose over audible parlance, that syntax of coils and twists left by the leader for one who follows—feathery Frost-knots, fluid water-knots and double figure-eights, tied-off uncertainties and plain-talking prusiks. The Incas used runners to move their *quipus*, their knot-messages from one spot to the next, and I do too, no disdainer of tradition. So on it goes, moving leechlike on two eight-foot slings, one probing forward before the other is plucked from behind. Ever falling forward in faith, yet only because of ties to what's known and certain. . . .

No knot-talking with anyone today; not-talking. Must've tied more knots on that five-day cooking gig on the Kodiak king-crab boat than in all my days of climbing. Never heard the polyphonous song of knots before that rolling day at sea, that time of fixing nets and trying to break their encrusted code, struggling high above the deck to wrest from gaps and fringes the pattern that once was.

AH, the rhythm has returned: first perusal of outlying reaches, then grasping and rasping upward, spliced spasms of extension and contraction like quickly coiling an endless rope. Yes, there's been that certain sense of correctness ever since the pointed gesture of the ptarmigan; now, as then, a route with sweeping surety and compelling logic in its line—there is no debate or hesitation, no sense of commitment; it is obvious, clear, and inevitable. No creation or control, nothing of the sort.

Quite a short blockish face with slender cracks. The powder snow gleams now, it's bronze, brass, now goldleaf. But wait...of course! the sun's on its way down over Samvega to the west, a brilliant solarizing process coating silver over all, a darkroom technique. Bivi? Nary a spot to even sit down, no down booties, Salvation Army surplus wool tweeds from Spokane, down parka—ah, for a feather shirt like the Eskimo, and a caribou parka. It doesn't look good. Certain snow again from WNW, falling flakes already; better fly to the top and then down. No time for protection, slings below around the neck now, the snow cackles and burns brightly as it ushers in the twilight's flatness, so climb! Gracefully, with certainty and aplomb....

No responsibility. None at all. No knots or cords to bind me despite mid-fifth-class terrain, chimneying up behind an enormous block right to its crest, wondering if it will lurch, no. Stretch taut all sinew now, reach for that knob, loose but not free, hoist again, and full weight on those holds—lugs up! to grab with rubber teeth. Moving swiftly, lightly, completely, thoughts woven into willow baskets hold back the doubt, stowed out of sight. Gravity's attraction is nil: perhaps it is always this way. Relaxed, like lying in the pews, dozing in the sandstone Church of the Covenant in Boston last May, listening to that sweet all-night jazz until breakfast, a stream of music to move by; never did catch the name of that last group.

The angle's down, all fourth class, pitch or two now to the crest. Hello! other side; my, you boast fine glacier tongues nearby, and the same gentle sheep tracts on meadowy south sides; a definite summit in the last falling light. The Inukshuk valley hosts a flotilla of clouds steaming this way, storms from the arctic seas just at the horizon, polar bergs and bears almost within sight.

There was a bare, bleached-bone honesty in that valley, wide and clear.

SUMMER & WINTER ASCENTS
DENNIS SCHMITT

Off and on I have been somewhat of a mountaineer in the Brooks Range for ten years now since I was nineteen. Yet even as a very young child I had dreams of a range of mountains somewhere so far north that the Big Dipper and the North Star stood above them at the zenith of the sky, a mountain range that formed a magical ring around the North Pole and protected Santa Claus from such pedestrian influences as the Fourth of July. When I first saw a map of the Brooks Range in my later childhood I immediately took them to be these same mountains. Moreover I took them to be a concretely logical extension of the hills in my backyard making their way north along the Pacific border of the American continent. You may be sure that by the time I had at last arrived in Anaktuvuk Pass, a Nunamiut Eskimo village in the middle of the Brooks Range, in 1965, I had already dreamt my way into their fabled midst many times over. And I can say, without reservation, that the age-old dreamer within me was vindicated by what he beheld—a landscape for which I felt an instant nostalgia, a landscape that inspired deep within me a terrible longing never to die, never to go blind to the world, a landscape of beautiful people magically different from myself, as true a fairy tale as ever I have witnessed on this earth.

All through the late summer, fall, and early winter of that year I focused my energies toward adapting to Nunamiut village life, learning to handle the dog teams, to kill, skin, and prepare meat, to gather willow fuel, to speak the language, to mend my Tannik (white man's) personality, and to look only passively around at the horizon, inhibiting any mountaineering ambitions I might have Then late in February, when life was very difficult, the men and dogs having left the village in a desperate search for caribou, and the women and children having merged households to consolidate body heat and conserve fuel, I suddenly felt the urge to escape from village life into the world of the pyramids and pinnacles above me.

Three miles north of the village was Peak 5,280, gleaming in the noon twilight. "Things couldn't be much worse up there," I thought, "at least there's a little sunlight in the middle of the day." Perhaps too I thought of impressing the Nunamiut a bit with my spirit of adventure in the already brutal face of things. Hearing of my plans for an ascent they, however, assured me that whatever the outcome they would not be impressed whatsoever. In the blowing snow, mist, and darkness of that same afternoon I was pulling a sled-load of ice with an older Nunamiut man near the graveyard north of the village. He warned me that if I should die on the mountain I would be buried as unmomentously and cheaply as possible and be entirely forgotten by spring. He showed me how hard the frozen ground was to dig. Pointing out a possible plot for myself, only half in jest, I told him that I would nevertheless be careful. He thanked me, though I knew how dearly he would, in truth, enjoy seeing a Tannik dead. He was the sort of man who saw human mortality as an opportunity for revenge against his enemies rather than as a threat to himself. He loved to play with the vocabulary of death, both in English and Eskimo, and continued in that manner, despite the dark and wind, all the way back to the village.

The equipment by which I would either live or die on this ascent was Paleolithic in the best sense of the word. I had brought some fine caribou calf skins from hunting in the eastern mountains while living in a Kutchin village the summer before. Two beautiful Nunamiut girls and their observant mothers helped me prepare these skins and cut and sew them into a parka and pants. An older, more occasionally divine lady made me some caribou-skin boots for a good price, and another lady with as sweet a soul as God ever conceived, completed my outfit with inner socks and mittens. She was shedding tears for me as I put on my satchel and makeshift, soft-bound skis to set out for the base of Peak 5,280. This peak is called Suakpuk (big scold) by the Nunamiut (the Geological Survey map designates Peak 5,883, four miles to the west, as Suakpuk. Such discrepancies are entirely usual in much of Alaska). It is a startlingly dramatic peak and is composed of great walled layers of nearly horizontal limestone which constitute the predominating formation in this part of the range. Its southern buttress, an exquisite limestone pyramid, dominates the village as a cathedral dominates a medieval European city. North of the pyramid lie two steeply ridged gullies and then the imposing, vertical limestone walls of the northeastern face. The summit is a series of pinnacles, the southernmost being the highest.

High at the base of the south gully I left my skis and discovered that my wolf-dog, Shillig, had followed my trail and would soon be upon me. I waited for her as I checked my equipment, which was limited to my clothing, a thermometer, dried meat, cookies, and an old camera. The snow was very dry and I knew I would be thirsty before long. Shillig and I proceeded up the deep snows of the gully, moving toward the right-hand ridge until, at an altitude of less than 4,000 feet, we were climbing up the buttresses and chimneys of the ridge proper. The separate ascents of some of these buttresses involved technical difficulties, although vertical exposures were not more than forty feet. I proved to be Shillig's vehicle for much of the route—I climbed with her over my shoulders. Occasionally I had to throw her bodily up a face to ledges where I left her clinging and howling desperately as I made my own way. On one occasion, as she stood on my shoulders, I was on the verge of losing my footing on a wall of conglomerate. "Get up and jump! Jump, Shillig, jump!" I cried as I began to slip. And she did indeed jump as I fell, bruising my shoulders and knees and at last crashing against a steep wall of hard snow. I brushed the snow out of my neck and looked up to see her forty feet above me, gazing down disconsolately and silently. "Well, you got the best of that one," I told her. As we started again, the snow was getting harder, and we were buffeted more and more by the winds of the summit ridge. In the high wind, climbing on the hard-packed snows of the ridge proved very treacherous with my caribou-skin bottoms and I suffered many helpless falls. The summit was reached by traversing an exposed ledge beneath an overhang. From the summit I gazed down on the limestone pyramid forming the south rampart of the mountain and could see the village beyond and far below. "So that is where I have been living all this time," I said to myself, "I would never really have known where it was otherwise." The village itself appeared as an inadvertent exception to the arctic nothingness that engulfed it. I imagined how pitiful I might appear to a god or a spaceman (or even a Wien Airlines pilot, for that matter) looking down from a little higher still.

It was minus 29 degrees F. and as the wind was continuing to rise, I could not long contemplate the landscape. I left in twilight and high winds, working my way into the protected hollows of the eastern face. Even in descending, I had to be very careful to avoid any exertion that might frost my lungs. On a milder note, however, there was surprisingly little risk of avalanche due to the dry winter climate of this region and I was able to use avalanche chutes in making my descent. At the base of the mountain the weather had turned extremely cold and a strong north wind almost literally blew me back into the village. There I drank my tea, ate my food, and graciously let myself be reacquainted with the warm bathtub of village life.

South of the village lies an eloquent valley called Inukpuk or Great Spirit. It is dominated by a pyramid, Peak 4,850, with a steep, fluted north face. This valley and peak had intrigued my mountaineering sensibilities for some time, and one afternoon as I was scraping sheep skins and looking out the window at the peak, I received another warning. The Nunamiut lady who had made my mittens told me darkly, "*No one ever* went *that* way (up that mountain) . . . you really shouldn't go away that way again." She did not speak English and I had always felt that accounted in some measure for the exquisite gentility of her nature. I told her that I had terrible doubts about the mountain myself, but that I might go anyway just to spite myself. The next morning I told her to look for sunlight on the summit not long after noon. I left the village, alone in darkness with a north wind at my back and the temperature at minus 28 degrees F., carrying in my satchel leather climbing boots, food, water, a camera, and a mirror. I reached the base of the north face directly under the summit. From here the face appeared much steeper and longer than it had earlier. I was apprehensive and exhilarated as I began to climb, sensing my whole life flickering about me in all its transient detail. I made my way up the very steep ridge to the left of the chute leading to the obvious notch east of the summit. From an altitude of 3,000 feet I was forced to climb difficult fourth class chimneys and a few very exposed buttresses. I found myself all but trapped at many junctures. The ascent would not have been possible without climbing boots and was not reasonable without ropes. The latter fact made for a richly emotional climb. As many times as I found myself cramped against the edge of oblivion, I found myself also falling in love with some new female from out of my past. On the summit, after tunneling through a cornice, I forgot all this and settled back into my skin boots to warm my frozen feet. I found a cairn there and a note of previous ascent by Steven Porter, a geologist, on "July first, 1959, via the east ridge in hail and snow." So my Nunamiut friend had been mistaken; someone else had been up here.

The temperature on the summit was minus 31 degrees F. I took out my mirror and reflected a glimmer of the low afternoon sunlight into the village, verifying both my success and survival. Just then, in a misty temperature inversion over Inupuk Valley, I thought I saw the face of a laughing man out of the corner of my eye. Yet when I looked at it straight on it was gone.

The descent down the steep, very hard wind-blown snow of the west ridge was very treacherous. To return to the village I had to battle my way north along the bare ice of the river against forty to sixty mile winds. The ground visibility was totally obscured by blowing snow, and yet above me great waves of aurora loomed throughout the black sky between the mountain walls. As blinded as I was, I felt utterly blessed in that I was nevertheless not utterly blind.

In the spring that followed these first winter ascents I began to move freely about the landscape, traveling by whim for days at a time with only such food as I could catch along the way. My mountaineering even proved useful to the Nunamiut when I was able to climb into the clouds, find the caribou and coax them down into ambush on group hunting expeditions. Roaming about in the fogs of the upper slopes I acquainted myself, furthermore, with every form of mammal known to that region. I ignored, however, the summits. For the time being I felt I had learned whatever they had to teach.

A few years later I was berry picking with some Nunamiut women and children in Inukpuk Valley under the north face of Peak 4,850 when one lady pointed the mountain out to me. "You hear what someone says," she smiled, "someone says *that* mountain is *Dennis Mountain, Ekkayoak* (my Eskimo name) *Mountain! You...*" I saw the pyramid reflected in her eyes and realized finally what she had said. "My mountain," I said tentatively. "My mountain!" I cried with greater assurance, gazing blankly into space with a feeling the pharaohs must have felt. "Ekkayoak, Ekkayoak Mountain is better than Dennis Mountain," I said matter of factly. "It's all temporary, of course, but still Ekkayoak is much, much better than Dennis as a name for a mountain." At which time the lady suddenly broke out into laughter, wild, playful laughter. "I jokes," she said, "I jokes you real good on that time. You think someone can give you the mountain. Even Nunamiut can't do that." At that I paused, reflected, and collapsed in dismay. And so it was that Peak 4,850, as if in a comedian's dream, brought me within a breath of immortality but did not let me stick. Of course, nowadays who knows whose mountain it is. I truly believe I was up there once, but it's getting harder and harder to remember. □

Illustrations by Allison Clough

THE EIGER
TWO PERSPECTIVES

Left: At the base of the White Spider
Right: Hinterstoisser Traverse
Toni Hiebeler photos

A CLIMB
CHRIS KOPCZYNSKI

However good he may be, and however favorable the conditions of his ascent, anyone who returns from the Eigerwand cannot but realize that he has done something more than a virtuoso climb: he has lived through a human experience to which he had committed not only all his skill, intelligence and strength, but his very existence.

Lionel Terray

THE SUN HAD SET and the entire Alai Valley was overcast with thunder and lightening. I rolled over in my sleeping bag and gazed through the tent flaps into a gray-black sky. A cold and crisp wind shook the tent.

I was one of eighteen Americans on the 1974 International Expedition to the Pamirs. We experienced terrible weather and witnessed one of the worst tragedies in the history of mountaineering. In two days we would pack our climbing gear and head for home.

"Kop, come over here!"

The command was John Roskelley's and came from the adjacent tent. Pulling on my coat and boots, I walked to his tent and poked my head through the opening. There sat Roskelley, motionless beneath a single light bulb.

"Come on in, Chris, let's talk." I crawled inside and sat on a rucksack.

"Kop, let's go to Switzerland and try the Eiger. You know I'm looking for a partner, and I'd like you to go." I had realized before leaving the States that Roskelley had an extension fare to Switzerland and was planning to attempt something big. I was speechless; the answer was going to take a lot of thinking.

"Look, John, there's a bit of a problem. I don't have a ticket, and I'm expected home in a week."

"Think it over, Kop, and let me know in a couple of days. You can switch tickets with John Marts. You know you can find a way if you want to."

"Okay, I'll think about it—see you in the morning." I crawled out into the icy air and plunged into my own tent and cold bag. Later, I woke up in a cold sweat, dreaming that I was on the Second Icefield of the Eigerwand.

The morning of our departure, Roskelley approached me again. My decision had taken much deliberation, but now I was ready. "Yeah, John, I'm going." I was committed now. We would give it a try.

Saying farewell to the ill-fated Pamir camp was easy as we rode away in army trucks. On arrival in Moscow twenty-four hours later, I got a phone connection to Seattle. This was going to be my first problem—telling my wife!

"Sharon! I'm going to Switzerland for a week—I'll be home later than planned!"

"What? Who is this?"

I yelled through the phone for fear of her not hearing me. There was dead silence for thirty seconds and the thought of the eight-dollar-a-minute toll charge raced through my mind.

"I'm going to Switzerland!"

"WHAT? Chris, is that you?"

Later, Roskelley and I arrived in Zurich and optimistically purchased round-trip tickets to the Bernese Oberland.

We awoke early the next morning in Grindelwald, a resort town a few miles from the mountain. Planning for three nights out, we packed carefully and lightly, taking no stove and only lunch-type foods. Since my camera was smaller and lighter, I talked John into leaving his behind. Once on board the train to Kleine Scheidegg, Roskelley relaxed and puffed a cigar.

It was early afternoon as John started upward over fourth class rock. I couldn't help noticing all the water running over the rock—it was only a taste of things to come. For 500 feet we ascended steadily—finally I demanded the rope. John grumbled but agreed. Five hundred feet higher we reached the Difficult Crack, the beginning of the serious climbing. Since water was flowing heavily down the crack, John was forced into gymnastics to avoid a drenching. I decided to stay dry by jumaring on

Eigerwand/Swiss Nat'l Tourist Office

the blank wall to the right. This worked fine for forty feet, until I was forced into the water; in thirty seconds I was semi-drenched.

Three more leads brought us to a series of narrow, horizontal ledges beneath the Rote Fluh, a huge, blank wall. This was the start of the infamous Hinterstoisser Traverse. It looked worse than I had ever imagined, and it remains in my mind as one of the hardest sections of the climb.

Roskelley fixed the rope to a couple of ancient ring pegs and pounded in a good one of his own as he traversed out onto the black rock, water pouring down upon him and his rucksack. The scene from my perch was incredible: I watched John traverse slightly down and out of sight on what appeared to be absolutely nothing.

Twenty minutes later I heard a faint "Belay On!" through the roar of water. I will never forget that traverse. Water streamed over the black rock and the holds were small wrinkles which only got smaller as I progressed. All the stories about the Eiger pioneers raced through my mind, and it became very apparent why the wall has claimed so many lives. Only John's "Hurry up, redneck" spread warmth on the frightful surroundings.

From a small stance in a chimney, John led straight up for a full pitch and soon shouted down that he had reached the Swallow's Nest, a favorite and historical bivouac site. My elation was shortlived, for when I reached the Nest I found water dripping heavily on the only decent sleeping place. John was crouched off to the left, on a small, downsloping patch of ice only a few feet from the First Icefield.

"Welcome to the Swallow's Nest Annex," commented Roskelley. This was our first bivouac.

The weather had been unstable throughout the day and now turned to a gray drizzle. As the rain grew heavier, the run-off from the First Icefield grew to a large torrent. Stones began to buzz overhead in flurries, and although nothing was said, we both thought of retreat at daylight. The rain stopped after a few hours and we passed a somewhat restful night.

By daybreak we were numb—with much apprehension we strapped on crampons for the ascent of the First Icefield. The next few hours would be the most exposed to stonefall. The first lead ended at a treacherous spot on fifty-five degree ice, with stones buzzing all around us. Up went John again on frontpoints, axe, and hammer. Lifting my eyes from under my helmet, I watched as he reached the base of the Ice Hose (or Water Hose!). I made my way to the belay and the security of its overhang just as another barrage of rocks crashed down.

"Where to from here?" The Ice Hose was definitely out of condition, and I was surprised to see that it was nearly vertical—I had supposed it to be about sixty degrees. John led up carefully, so as not to dislodge any more stones than were already falling, some the size of pumpkins. At forty feet, climbing up and over a difficult overhang, he was out of sight.

Crack!!

"Roskelley, what's goin' on?

"A rock split my helmet!"

John admitted later that at that point he was ready to rappel. The three leads which followed were over intensely difficult ground with shingle-type, layered rock. Water ran everywhere. At last we reached the base of the impressive Second Icefield, where three leads straight up black ice took us to the bergschrund and safety from falling rock. Except for the distant whirr of stones, the face once again appeared peaceful. We relaxed for a few minutes and listened to cowbells far below. The sky had finally cleared.

The ascent now became enjoyable—we traversed four full pitches across the top of the Second Icefield to the cliff below the Flatiron. Three leads of moderate climbing led to the notorious Death Bivouac. We paused here for a much-needed rest and ate a late lunch. Off to the left lay the Third Icefield, the steep passage to the Ramp.

As again we struck out onto the ice, a barrage of stones shot past.

"We got to move fast, Kop."

"I'm going as fast as I can," I bluntly replied.

With the aid of picks and frontpoints, we reached the safety of the Ramp. Here the worst of the stonefall ended. We moved quickly up the Ramp for 450 feet—it felt solid and safe underfoot. The Ramp is a chimney system completely protected from falling stones and water. The chimney narrows eventually to a crack which we figured would be the crux of the entire climb.

At the top of the Ramp we sat on a two-foot-wide ledge beneath the crack, which had water pouring down it. There was only one way to go—straight up the crack. Roskelley argued that it would be better to get wet then than in the morning, and so after climbing for a few minutes he was soaked to the skin. I watched as the water poured down his legs and gushed into his boots. His toes had been severely frostbitten in 1973, but not a word came from him as he slowly progressed. I knew the pain was excruciating. Finally he manteled onto the ledge at the brink of the waterfall, and I heard a low, agonized, "I'm up, Kop, get ready."

I stripped and stuffed all my semi-dry clothing into my rucksack. I glanced downward—far below, the clouds were gathering as the sun set, coloring the horizon with brilliant pinks and oranges. I heard the clang of a cowbell and the bark of a dog drifting up from an invisible pasture, and I was flooded with peace. Turning my gaze upward to the overhanging waterfall, however, brought me back to reality. Moving off the exposed stance, I shivered in the freezing air and ascended as fast as the jumars would bite the rope. Removing the pins ended in utter frustration—I too was totally drenched.

Reaching John, I found him with his boots off.

"How are your feet, man?"

"They're wet but okay. My hands are still numb."

Top of the Second Icefield/Chris Kopczynski

Exit Cracks/*Kopczynski*

The sun had set and except for the lights of Grindelwald and a few other towns in the Oberland, all was dark. We were fortunate in having good weather; nevertheless, we spent a rather miserable night shivering to keep warm, since every piece of clothing we had was soaked.

At the first sign of daybreak we prepared our wet gear and tried to warm our hands for what we hoped would be our final hours on the face. John led out to the left, then went straight up verglas-covered rock. He had to continually blow on his hands, and I realized that the pace was to be agonizingly slow. Fifteen feet above me he came to a short, overhanging section. With infinite delicacy and poise he crawled upward and over. On a small stance just above this, he strapped on his crampons. When fifty feet of rope was out, it stopped, played out a few more feet, then dribbled back into my lap.

"Chris! I have to take off my pack. I'll tie it to the wall, and you can tie both sacks onto the rope when you reach here."

Twenty minutes passed before I finally heard, "Belay Off." He had made it past the frozen waterfall known as the Ice Bulge. The ascent up this section was the most difficult ice climbing on the Eigerwand. Just below John I shamelessly went hand over hand up the rope to the stance.

"Let's move, man."

"What the hell do you think I've been trying to do?"

Steep ice alternating with belts of bad rock finally brought us to the beginning of the fabled Traverse of the Gods. Although scary, the traverse was not difficult, and we soon reached the base of the White Spider. This icefield, in bad conditions, catches all the frequent avalanches which sweep the upper face. Luckily, the weather held.

Above the Spider, we traversed up and left into the first Exit Crack. Roskelley moved cautiously up cracks and overhangs, and after much deliberation and delicate climbing, reached a small, finger-like projection known as the Pedestal. Securing our own rope, and hooking into an old one, we rappelled to the base of a wide chimney. We followed this for over 400 feet.

The chimney behind us, the angle eased, and we ascended several leads on down-sloping rock which brought us to the summit icefield. The North Face was below us. The problem now was to get down the west flanks in the remaining light.

A FILM
CHIC SCOTT

What's it all about? Where do you lose that youthful dream, that idealism?

Maybe on this page....

Or maybe not.

Perhaps I'll know by the time I reach the end.

Rébuffat has written, "Youth, to live, must have some great aspiration. When I was fifteen... I longed so much to become a mountaineer and one day, perhaps, a guide!"

How long it seems since I read that.

In this era of climbing commercialism, it is a little difficult to retain any integrity. The lure of glistening, distant peaks has been replaced by the lure of gold and silver, and it seems as if no climber can resist. Now Hollywood is in the arena, with the resources to make a Judas of any of us.

For seven weeks during the summer of 1974 I worked on the filming of *The Eiger Sanction*. It was a miserable time. It is over now and I am glad. But the summer lives on in more than memories, and that is what this... (confession?) is all about.

For most of us mountaineers working on the film, it was our *Fistful of Dollars*. To one who lived on pea soup and porridge in a shepherd's hut, it was a home for his wife and child. To another it was a log cabin in Wyoming, and to another it was the break into a new life as a professional mountaineer.

For me it was my temptation, my thirty days in the wilderness.

I had qualms about accepting the job. The smiling face of Toni Kurz, and the struggles of Heckmair and the rest were my boyhood treasures; the *White Spider* was my Homerian epic.

But who among us can resist the lure of Hollywood, the silver screen, the starlets and the wine—and the money? I justified it by convincing myself that I might be able to get the whole script rewritten...(In the face of the storm the team pulls together, and espionage and murder are forgotten. Through the Eiger's most bitter mood, an international team wins through to the top. Friends and heroes, the team descends, and the culprit is found elsewhere—as does happen in the book.)

Fat chance.

Juggling greed and idealism, and scared silly of what I might have to do, I made my annual flight east.

Two pleasant days were spent scouting the face and rigging. "That scene on the Shattered Pillar would be terrific, and the cameraman could film from the 3.8 km. window. The Rote Fluh is steep, too steep for actors, but it's safe." I learned a lot and made a fine acquaintance with the mountain. On the third day we started shooting.

My first task was a twenty-five foot leap into space and I balked. A somewhat dramatic scene in the brass and leather Scheidegg Hotel bar the night before, and my cover was blown. I spoke my piece. No falls! But, of course, there were others more anxious than I that the show go on, and the gap was filled.

Another point was raised that night—how many people would be killed by showing the wrong techniques and attitudes? I won few friends but made my point. That was the last official meeting, and our after-dinners were undisturbed in the future.

I was relegated to other duties off camera.

And so the film rolled.

Two days later, at nightfall, we flew to a cliff high on the Eiger's west ridge. The body of one of the team hung jackknifed in space, suspended from the anchor rope. My mind could barely register, for it was all too real. There was nothing we could do. His dreams of a Scottish Highland cottage were gone forever.

In climbing there are too many scenes that you can't retake. We had spent two days rigging and shooting the most difficult part of the film: "Stonefall hits climber who is held on rope and then pulled onto ledge. Climber ultimately dies." All had gone well and the final scene (plastic rocks being dropped from above) had been shot when a real rock did its job. Result: one dead real climber and one bruised cameraman.

We all know one thing—climbing is very real and Hollywood is fantasy. You can't forget that and stay alive. I had been standing beside my now-dead friend twenty minutes before it happened and, as I was no longer needed, excused myself and jumared to the waiting helicopter. It was the second spookiest place I have ever been.

They say that the show must go on and it did. After a few days grace and the miraculous appearance of a special $100,000 insurance policy, we were back at it—bivouac scenes, ice climbing, rockclimbing, and day-for-night

The film team/*John Cleare*

ILLUSION AND REALITY

PHOTOS BY JOHN CLEARE

shots with knives flickering in the moonlight as they silently slit ropes (oh, sacred ropes). But the heights of absurdity and black humor had yet to be plumbed, and several days were spent doing the "body-hauling scene." Bidet, the body, was not real and became a silent companion. The humor was that a rope continually oozed real blood on wet snow. No one ever considered replacing it.

Finally we reached the "body-discovered scene." The make-up man outdid himself and created a frozen, putrid, and mutilated corpse. We all remember Longhi, Sedlmayer, and Mehringer and so, it seems, did the scriptwriter.

Ironically, at this point someone commented that the movie had lost all contact with reality.

Finally there was the dramatic leap, the three-thousander down the face—the ultimate peel. Even my California cousins balked at this, and so three dummies were enlisted. Footage from cameras thrown over the edge and from several dozen other falls should make a heart-stopping climax.

There was some climbing for fillers. The Shattered Pillar was never touched, although it offered, to me, the finest camera angles for climbing. The actors did most of their paces themselves on an assortment of cliffs and boulders.

Several more serious moves were recorded with stunt men in "doubling gear," but they should not consume too much of the public's time.

So if that's the film, then what of the people?

A mixture and, surprisingly, a pleasant one.

The First Assistant Director liked the mountains, hiked with his wife and took some pleasure in learning a little technical climbing. He was always helpful and a joy to be with.

The Chief Cameraman made it fifty feet off the ground for the day-for-night shot and must have discovered more than camera angles. Perhaps it was the sunny weather, the meadows, the cowbells, and the light on the Jungfrau, for that night he ecstatically thanked us for the finest day of his life.

George Kennedy could not leave Scheidegg soon enough, although he was always most personable. He knew that mountains were for mountaineers, and that he was an actor (a good one, the best of the group).

Jean-Pierre Bernard had the roles straight and did a fine job for the cameras. He knew that climbing is for climbers, and every day on the mountain was a test for him. Anyway, who wants to play a cuckolded, middle-aged has-been who gets bonked on the head and then dragged all over a mountain?

Michael Grimm showed the most climbing aptitude and has moved to Austria, where he hikes and skis with his family. Perhaps he is a little weak on his lines, but climbers were never much for words.

And Reiner, six-foot-five Reiner. Well, he lives every role he plays, so who knows?

Finally there's Clint, .44 Magnum traded for an ice axe. Eastwood, like the character he played, was willing to take his chances with the Eiger. They both lived through it, but not because of their own doing. Perhaps the gods look out for those without consciences, but who try. He's got a lot more nerve and energy than I have, but I would not trade places.

The real and pretend Eigerpeople: Clint Eastwood, Reinhold Messner, Heidi Buhl, and Peter Habeler. *J. J. Rayman photo.*

Through it all, the parade of Eiger candidates passed by. Messner and Habeler made their astounding ten-hour ascent. Roskelley and Kopczynski came and went as most, unnoticed.

I played on the fringes, vacillating between guilt and despair. In late September the mountain was left to itself, and the party went home.

Who knows what will end up on the cutting-room floor and what will make the screen? It is unlikely, but there may be some taste shown in the editing.

One thing is certain—this summer Eastwood will again be the North American idol, and the two fellows who climbed the face for real will go unheralded. But perhaps that is the way it should be.

And for the future, another film is being discussed. It will be on the life of Gary Hemming. Perhaps if the folks from Hollywood look closely enough into that life and themselves, they may realize why he blew his brains out. □

The north face in winter/*Swiss Nat'l Tourist Office*

BOOKS

OF THE MANY recently published books concerned with mountaineering, only a few stand out as exceptional; many are flawed through mundane writing and/or poor photographic reproduction. Yet all these books have something to offer, and *Ascent* has selected for review a representative sample of nineteen titles which can be placed into four departments: Autobiographies, Guidebooks, Explorations and Expeditions, and General.

As usual, the Europeans continue to churn out autobiographies in rapid succession. Two of the grand old men of mountaineering history, Edmund Hillary and Anderl Heckmair, offer us their memories of climbing as it used to be, as well as describing their changing views toward life and death. A leading alpinist of the 1950s, Walter Bonatti, and the present-day *wunderkind* Reinhold Messner not only describe their epic adventures, but write of their concerns for a fast-growing sport. It is perhaps significant that most of the reviewers of these autobiographies note that there is far too little in them about the author's real feelings and virtually nothing about their relationships with their partners and friends.

Of the guidebooks reviewed, two concern themselves with small Western rockclimbing areas. The Sierra Club's long-awaited guide to the High Sierra is finally completed and available for the summer hordes. A strange "guidebook" to Mt. McKinley and a stunning production from the prolific Gaston Rébuffat complete the section.

The three books in the Explorations and Expeditions section take us to two of the earth's wildest places, Patagonia and the Himalaya.

It is in the final section that we find the books that refuse to be categorized. Warren Harding, the legendary Yosemite cragsman, has written a fascinating and outrageous book which will be talked about for some time. Chris Jones began his monumental tome while recovering from a major ski injury in 1972—the book took a little longer than he thought, but he has come up with a comprehensive volume which puts him in the estimable position of being an author with a big, important book *and* a leader of present-day alpinism (see page 8). The only instruction book reviewed this year is Ruth and John Mendenhall's latest work—they have been involved in climbing and writing for over forty years. Four British books close out the reviews. Ken Wilson, long associated with *Mountain*, gives us a selection of the finest British rock climbs as seen through leading climber/writers. The books by Walt Unsworth, John Cleare, and Doug Scott have in common their grandiose titles. Scott, like Chris Jones, knows what he's talking about; he recently climbed Mt. Everest by the oft-tried southwest face.

THE TITLES

Nothing Venture, Nothing Win, by Sir Edmund Hillary. New York: Coward, McCann & Geohegan, 1975. 319 pages. $12.95.

My Life as a Mountaineer, by Anderl Heckmair. London: Victor Gollancz Ltd., 1975. 224 pages. £4.50. Translated by Geoffrey Sutton from the German edition titled *Mein Leben als Bergsteiger,* 1972.

The Great Days, by Walter Bonatti. London: Victor Gollancz Ltd., 1974. Translated by Geoffrey Sutton. 189 pages. £3.80.

The Seventh Grade, by Reinhold Messner. New York: Oxford University Press, 1974. 160 pages.

Pinnacles Climber's Guide, by Chuck Richards. Santa Maria, California: Recreation and Travel Enterprises, 1974. 128 pages. $5.50.

Squamish Chief Guide, by Gordon Smaill. Vancouver: Bill Lupul and Marlene Smaill, 1975. 114 pages $4.50.

The Climber's Guide to the High Sierra, by Steve Roper. San Francisco: Sierra Club, 1976. 384 pages. $7.95.

Mount McKinley Climber's Guide, by Dennis Cowals. Anchorage: Alaska Alpine Co., 1976. $5.00.

The Mont Blanc Massif—The 100 Finest Routes, by Gaston Rébuffat. New York: Oxford University Press, 1974. 239 pages. $20.00.

Himalayan Odyssey, by Trevor Braham. London: George Allen & Unwin Ltd., 1974. 243 pages. $17.50.

Mountain of Storms, by Andrew Harvard and Todd Thompson. New York: Chelsea House, New York University Press, 1974. 210 pages.

Tierra del Fuego: the Fatal Lodestone, by Eric Shipton. London: Charles Knight & Co., Ltd., 1973. 175 pages. $13.75.

Downward Bound—A Mad Guide to Rock Climbing, by Warren Harding. New Jersey: Prentice-Hall, 1975. 204 pages. $7.95.

Climbing in North America by Chris Jones. Berkeley: University of California Press, 1976. 395 pages. $14.95.

Beginner's Guide to Rock and Mountain Climbing, by Ruth and John Mendenhall. Harrisburg, Pa.: Stackpole Books, 1975. 159 pages. $3.95.

Hard Rock: Great British Rock-Climbs, compiled by Ken Wilson. London: Hart-Davis, Macgibbon, 1975. 220 pages.

Encyclopaedia of Mountaineering, by Walt Unsworth. New York: St. Martin's Press, Inc., 1975. 272 pages $12.95.

Mountains, by John Cleare. New York: Crown Publishers, Inc., 1975. 256 pages. $12.50.

Big Wall Climbing, by Doug Scott. New York: Oxford University Press, 1974. 348 pages. $12.50.

THE REVIEWS

Nothing Venture, Nothing Win. When I first became interested in climbing, I read every expeditionary account and every biography of a climber that I could find. I did not notice most were poorly written, and I did not care when genuine suffering was covered in modesty, or sincere but egotistic motivations were only hinted at to preserve the image of harmony and accord. When as a climber, I could compare the actions and ascents of my peers to the stylized image of the mountaineer, I could see how much of what I read was simply a chronicle of events, with little to do with the humans involved. And at that point, I stopped reading mountaineering literature. Now I know that mountaineering has little to do with the events and everything to do with the people. Mountaineering could not attract and hold people so cogently if it did not attract and hold some primal element in them. It is not that I do not care to know of other climbers' experiences, I simply do not want to read any more recipes for shuffling loads to high camps, or descriptions of hard moves on death-dealing rockclimbs at the expense of knowing why the climber cares to be there in the first place.

So I began Edmund Hillary's autobiography, *Nothing Venture, Nothing Win,* with some apprehension. Here was the story of the most famous mountaineer and adventurer, the so-called conqueror of Everest, past his prime as a climber and looking back to tell it all. With so long a list of accomplishments, Hillary could write a chronicle of his adventures and leave it at that. But as I thought of all that Hillary had done and how long he had been involved in mountaineering, I became more interested in what he thought and felt. Hillary has engaged in many forms of the adventurer-mountaineer—ideals that, to my mind, are contrasts. He was an inauspicious beginner but, with Tenzing Norgay, was the first to reach the summit of Everest. He was a loner, yet became the leader of many expeditions. He spent over a decade in the forefront of Himalayan climbing but also drove a tractor across the Antarctic ice to the South Pole. He has spent much humanitarian effort building hospitals, schools, and airstrips for the Sherpas while also working as a businessman for Sears.

Nothing Venture, Nothing Win is like most other climbers' autobiographies—it is a tolerably written adventure story. In chronologic order Hillary describes his explorations and adventures, and, perhaps because he waited until his fifties to write his autobiography, he gives a picture of himself that includes his family and business concerns. What he does write of his and others' talents and weaknesses is candid, but I sense many internal changes took place because of his climbing and fame that he does not mention. Often Hillary indicates something important or disturbing happened that affected his life without revealing exactly what it was or its effect. At the end of the book, he indicates his life has been strung together by a series of friendships. I believe him, but his portrayals of his friends and friendships have no depth. Also at the end of the book, Hillary states he feels a vast dissatisfaction for not taking advantage of all opportunities opened to him. I cannot believe he only recently felt that way, yet I cannot remember him mentioning it earlier in the book. Somewhere in *Nothing Venture, Nothing Win* Hillary describes a scene as unbelievably emotional, and then states he suppresses his own feelings with difficulty. Perhaps the desire to suppress his feelings is the reason so little of his personality comes through in his book. I would not argue that there are not occasions when it is best to suppress one's feelings, but they *should* be expressed in an autobiography.

In a recent interview Hillary speaks of his climbing and his life with a greater warmth and humor than he does in *Nothing Venture, Nothing Win*. I feel I have had only a glimpse of Hillary. He seems estimable, strong-willed, and likable. But having read his autobiography I should be able to say I know more. It is unfortunate that mountaineers seem unable to write freely of their internal motivations and searchings. Maybe mountaineers do not want to know so much about themselves. **Roger Breedlove**

My Life as a Mountaineer. Until Doug Scott's *Big Wall Climbing* appeared in 1974, not much had appeared in the English language concerning the development of climbing in the twenties and thirties. (Messner was once quoted as commenting that "modern Alpinism's greatest period was in the thirties.") Indeed, the historians who wrote in English were most antagonistic toward the Germans and Italians who were doing the great routes in the Eastern Alps, obviously due to the rise of both nationalism and mechanization . . . small wonder that Comici, Solleder and even Heckmair are not mentioned (possibly out of ignorance?). Who can forget Ullman's comments in *The Age of Mountaineering* (1941): "by the thirties the Alps were full of glory-seeking young climbers who looked down with contempt on anything less than a certified Super-Sixth. The Eigerwand, the north wall of the Grandes Jorasses, the north and west faces of the Matterhorn and various of the rock pinnacles in the Dolomites achieved a notorious celebrity as 'impossible' ascents, and it was on them in particular that the new order of Alpine cragsmen concentrated and struggled—and often died."

It amuses me to this day that those "mechanized" alpinists who died on the Jorasses, the Eigerwand, or in the Dolomites were considered "suicidal" and their broken bodies almost obscene by these same historians, while Himalayan climbers (with their Sherpa porters, axes, crampons, ladders, and even oxygen) who meet disaster on Everest are treated with reverence (because they are English speaking?).

Heckmair entered the world of climbing with amazing energy and dedication. For a good part of his early life he was an unemployed landscape gardener (these were depression years, do not forget), and he and his friends often lived like vagabonds in the mountain huts (those who had jobs would bring up food), traveling to and from climbs by ski and bicycle. Very early, even before he became a climber, he had a fatalistic view of life: "I found it [death] quite natural and it in no way prevented all my thoughts and desires from inclining towards mountaineering." He lost many of his friends to climbing accidents, the most tragic being the personal discovery of his comrades Rittler and Brehm, who had fallen to their deaths during an attempt on the Jorasses.

He became a mountain guide in 1933, and after making the sixteenth ascent of Comici's route on the north face of the Cima Grande, began concentrating on the Eigerwand, which, of course, led to his historic ascent of the face with Harrer, Vörg and Kasparek. He writes with candor of the consequences of this climb, refuting rather well, in my opinion, the age-old allegations that he and his Eiger friends were voluntary "pawns" of Hitler and the Third Reich. Certainly, one could prove him guilty by association, for his acquaintance with Leni Riefenstahl brought him several times into close contact with Hitler himself:

> . . . to questions regarding our reception and decoration by Hitler I answered that just like anybody else we felt honored at being picked out of our obscure existence and presented to the most powerful man in Germany and at being decorated by him. It could have happened to a dancing bear. As young men with no interest in politics we had no way of seeing where Nazi policies were going to lead. Not until the outbreak of war did the real political situation become clear. Nevertheless, I replied, I could not blame people in other countries for thinking as they did. The Nazis did indeed build us up into such stars that people believed we had been backed and financially subsidized by the Party. However, that is simply not true.

After the war Heckmair is involved in many mountain journeys, including a visit to Hunza and a reconnaissance of the Batura Peaks in Pakistan. He is invited, along with Rebitsch, Harrer, and Erwin Schneider, to join the 1953 Nanga Parbat expedition, but, according to Buhl, all four decline to go because of the restrictive contracts Herrligkoffer asks them to sign. The book ends with his excursion to the United States and Mexico in 1965 for the purpose of climbing Mt. Waddington and the volcanoes of Mexico. The book is entertaining and Heckmair emerges as a very durable, intense person . . . whose interests range beyond the realm of hard climbing to the mountain cultures of other lands. On the occasion of a *Mountain* Magazine interview with Heckmair in July 1971, the editors of *Mountain* wrote:

> Today, 65-year-old Heckmair lives and works in the resort of Oberstdorf, southern Germany. It was here that we interviewed him, sipping bourbon in his timber-lined basement flat as he recounted his experiences. A lady friend translated, occasionally collapsing in laughter as the diminutive guide interjected some bawdy Bavarian expletive to stress a point. Heckmair's leathery face creased with mischief and enjoyment as the evening drew on. So the foxy little landscape gardener from Munich is now naturally and modestly coming to terms with his belated acclaim as one of the world's greatest mountaineers, his attitudes still simple and honest, unchanged by the endless controversy that has raged round his greatest climb.

We can wish him well in his declining years. **Allen Steck**

The Great Days. In a critical review of climbing literature appearing in *Ascent*, 1974, Dave Roberts convincingly argues that the great majority of climbing autobiographies are very poor. Roberts, a literature teacher at Hampshire College, quickly uncovers the two main weaknesses in what climbers write about themselves: predictability and shallowness. Walter Bonatti's autobiography, *The Great Days*, suffers from many of the weaknesses Roberts identifies, yet remains a most captivating book.

As Roberts points out, autobiographies tend to follow a predictable and deadly model, starting with adolescent infatuation with the mountains as an overcompensation for some sort of ineptness in and rebellion against school, sports, or parental relations. Next comes early poverty and crazy stunts, then the tiger days of the early twenties, then the discovery of a perfect climbing partnership, then fame, then marriage, then a mellowing period, a turning from the passion of climbing to the ease of travel and companionship. Of course, it is not simply the expected which deadens most climbing autobiographies. Literature has always dealt with much that can be forecast in life, including love, passion, friendship, hardship, and death. Yet, predictable subject matter which is also shallow is certain to make for poor literature.

Roberts shows several ways in which autobiographies are shallow, pointing to the fact that much is left unexamined by the authors or not examined in depth. There is no honest look at the meaning of climbing as a career; scant appraisal of the increasing unwillingness to take risks after marriage; thin or stereotyped treatment of climbing friendships, the magical affinity and love between climbers; and practically no discussion of the role of women in climbers' lives.

The Great Days, and its precursor *On The Heights*, suffer from precisely the problems Roberts identifies. *The Great Days* is an account, a running history, not an insightful reflection, into the experience of climbing. On marriage, Bonatti devotes one sentence, "There is a woman to whom I am linked by a true and mutual bond of love." One must look to the preface of *On The Heights* to locate Bonatti's initial climbing urges. These are predictably defiant and separatist: "Even as a child I always found it much easier to deal with nature than with men . . . I found myself floundering, bewildered and unprepared, amid the often underhanded methods used by men . . . So I fled to the mountains." In *The Great Days*, Bonatti still maintains this adolescent perspective on social affairs and "methods used by men". Ho hum, "humanity has changed and no longer knows how to live . . . mankind is falling into the . . . tyranny of collectivism which systematically objectifies people." On friendships, Bonatti's insight and feeling is thin. In a potentially moving and evocative moment with a mountain companion—a farewell to DeBiasi at the foot of the Matterhorn before a solo winter ascent of the north wall by a new route—Bonatti admits not knowing how to reply to a farewell hug: "Fearing to see him going away, I did not even have the courage to look back."

Yet, for all its failings as literature, particularly compared to the work of Patey's *One Man's Mountains* and John Menlove Edward's *Samson*, *The Great Days* by brute force calls up an admiration and lifts our spirit. We need not know the inner workings of Bonatti's marriage, the meaning of friendships forged by climbing or how climbing is chosen as a career, to be moved by the raw data of a remarkable climber's achievements. Data hardly ever speaks for itself, but the climbs of Bonatti, however plainly described by the author, speak of the enormous well of

love, energy, and courage within this man.

When Bonatti reaches the summit of the Matterhorn after completing his new ascent, and, weeping, embraces the summit cross, we realize it is not egomania which drives this man. It is a deep passion for heights. The same realization is ours as we read of Bonatti's ascent of the Walker Spur in winter. Five days of sleeplessness and −30°C temperatures would turn back or kill those motivated by competitive instincts. Bonatti's courage and energy is no more evident than in the tragic retreat from the central pillar of Fresnay on Mont Blanc. The strongest in a party of four Frenchmen and three Italians, Bonatti clearly risks his own life to save his companions; all except one eventually perish. There are other incidents in Bonatti's career which demonstrate his rare passion for life and the mountains. Two examples are descending the north face of the Eiger alone with a fractured rib or continuing with a first ascent of the Whymper Spur on the Grand Jorasses by knotting together ropes cut in five pieces during a rockfall.

In sum, *The Great Days* is not a great book, but we read on because it is an entirely convincing chronicle of one man's love, strength, and courage. We may wish Bonatti perceived more deeply, but there is no question that he believes and feels deeply. As a result, his climbs are "a token of love towards the mountains," as he hoped they would be. Bravo to Bonatti! **Tom Higgins**

The Seventh Grade. Before discussing *The Seventh Grade*, it is appropriate to review Messner's stature in the climbing world. I was first aware of Messner in 1969 when he arrived back in Chamonix after his solo ascent of the north face of *Les Droites*. This eight-hour sprint up the most feared mixed climb in the Alps was the sensation of the season. Later the same year he soloed the 3,000-foot Philipp-Flamm route on the Civetta; another achievement that stunned the alpine world. Further afield, Messner was equally inspired. Summit dashes on Nanga Parbat and Aconcagua were a prelude to his alpine-style ascent of Hidden Peak with Peter Habeler.

Messner made his reputation largely by repeating alpine climbs—but repeating them with finesse. It is not so much what he has achieved in the Alps that sets him apart, but the manner in which he has done it. While others struggled on multi-day epics, Messner made the bold strokes. He is the most original and forceful climber in the world today.

In *The Seventh Grade* Messner describes some dozen climbs and the thoughts and preparations that surrounded them. The descriptions are brief and repetitive, and the events blur together; if you have read a Messner description of one Dolomite climb . . . . Further, there is no insight into the companions we fleetingly meet, nor is there any indication when any of the climbs took place. It could all have been the same year as far as the reader can tell. The real interest in the book lies in the essays that counterpoint the descriptions. But there is also a problem here, because the translator has failed to draw important distinctions. For example, we read "The foremost climbers in the United States have for years endeavoured to make the first free ascents of the old and partly technical routes." By "partly technical" the translator presumably means "partly aid"; a crucial difference. Where Messner talks of a voluntary ban on "technical aids" we must assume he means bolts. The translation is also unclear where

Messner refers to what is here termed "non-competitive climbing." The reviewer believes that Messner means climbing where success is not the overriding motive; it is better to descend if to carry on would involve transgressing the agreed ground rules, i.e., use of bolts, siege climbing, etc. (When I told a leading French alpinist that Messner expounds non-competitive climbing, he jokingly replied: "That's because the competition is so far behind.")

Elsewhere Messner's meanings are clear, and all worth pondering. He says "I will have nothing to do with climbs depending upon expansion bolts. . . . If I could not get up without employing such methods, I was prepared to give up and leave the solution to others." This attitude could be used far more rigorously in America, although Messner has yet to come face to face with Yosemite's blank rock. He puts considerable emphasis on his training methods and concludes: "Extreme climbing is perhaps one of the few sports which have, as yet, not reached the limit and which leave open the way to the attainment of completely new standards." There is little doubt that if climbers trained as intensively as Olympic athletes, they would, as Messner has, achieve the seventh grade.

About Himalayan climbing Messner wrote: "Accompanied by a man like Peter Habeler, I would risk trying an 8000-metre peak, having an equal chance and less risk than attached to a great expedition with all its customary ballyhoo." This prophecy has already come true, and I offer the following Messnerism as a pointer to the future: "In order to advance in the scale of difficulties, the climber must take a voluntary step backwards as regards the use of artificial methods."

Although Messner's book is unexceptional, and reveals little about himself, it is must reading for all concerned with the limits of the sport. **Chris Jones**

Pinnacles Climber's Guide. "$5.50! For another little guidebook to the Pinnacles? They must be kidding. I'll just have to read enough right now to write a review. Surely I won't want to buy it."

With that first reaction, this new guidebook faced a 5.9 mental wall before I ever opened the cover. In the end, I plunked down my $5.50 and took the book home. Fact is, Chuck Richards has created a guidebook that is actually fun to read. In the all-too-dull world of guidebooks, that makes it a bargain at any price.

Unless you live in California, you may not recognize Pinnacles National Monument. It's an almost microscopic park south of Hollister that serves as a wintertime retreat for climbers from the San Francisco area. The winter days are pleasant and snow-free. For a further description, let Richards tell you:

> For many years, Pinnacles' lighthearted array of quick, jaunty climbs was mostly passed over and relegated to a second seat as the trend setters of the period uncoiled their ropes on more impressive conquests. The great walls and spires of Yosemite . . .the lofty, unfrequented summits of the Sierra . . .these were the beckoning calls that drew climbers away from the civilization of central California. Certainly, Pinnacles was close and handy when inhospitable weather or time limits kept the mountains at bay but its own day hadn't arrived yet. It lacked the long, clean lines to follow, the multiday ascents, and the great unexplored faces to temper mind and body. And it didn't have pitons.
>
> To climbers with cricked necks from studying aerial routes and with full gear slings of jingling armament, Pinnacles has always taken a bit of getting used to. The first complaint regularly was the routes were too short and second, for further discouragement, there weren't many good cracks for piton protection. Indeed, cracks are almost nonexistent and leads have to be protected with bolts, ethically shunned and taboo virtually everywhere else. So Pinnacles remained outside the mainstream of climbing, usually with only small, infrequent parties vying for its summits.
>
> Now however, Pinnacles is coming into its own. Largely through new trends and popularization of the sport, the Monument is becoming known as a bright, lively climbing area—one without intimidating walls, hard lines, or an equally hard cadre of resident climbers for newcomers to be wary of. Increasingly people are entering the sport not with an eye to high-flung pitches or lofty terror but as a fun pastime—a quick and lively outdoor experience. And for that style of climbing, Pinnacles is well suited. True, long routes and hard routes are here for those who want them but by far the bulk of the climbs are moderately rated or lower. Rather than spend most of a day on one route, parties at Pinnacles can savor a half-dozen or more, with time out for a mid-day picnic.

The average climb at Pinnacles hardly requires a guidebook for routefinding. You simply walk up to the rock and look for bolts. The only real purpose served by the guidebook is to give an indication how to find the most enjoyable climbs. This requires a good map and a few comments about the nature and difficulty of the climbs. For the most part, involved route descriptions are superfluous even for the less experienced climbers. Richards has supplied good maps, even photographs in some cases, adequate route descriptions, and a commentary that is both humorous and useful.

An example of the jaunty style of this guidebook is the best description one could ask for:

> **Teter-Tower**
> 5.7. First ascent: March 10, 1962 by Jim & Bob Smith, Ed Sutton, Ed Gammon, Al Timmons & Doug Wendt. Later it was climbed free.
> Here's the most descriptive pinnacle in the valley— the 9 meter pedestal sporting a 2 meter balancing ball. You'll find it a few meters right of Hidden Pinnacle at the end of the valley and below the rocky rise to the Yaks looming beyond. Climb the front (W) face from 2 pines where small chocks will work in the bottom crack. In the hollow above, climb to either side of the ball. Rappel bolt is on the right.

There are about 200 such descriptions in this fine little guide. Maybe it is worth that exhorbitant price, after all.
George Oetzel

Squamish Chief Guide. Forty miles north of Vancouver lies an enormous mass of granite called the Squamish Chief. During the past two decades rockclimbers have established about 150 routes on the vertiginous cliffs. Though the biggest wall is but 1,500 feet in height, the six Grade V routes and the two in the Grade VI category compare favorably with the great big-wall climbs of Yosemite Valley.

In the last few years more and more climbers have arrived at the Chief from afar and a guidebook was inevitable. In 1967 Glenn Woodsworth came out with an adequate, low-key guide, but a guidebook written then was soon destined to become quickly obsolete because of the explosion of new climbers and their routes. Gordon Smaill, a Canadian who has made his mark in Yosemite as well as on the Chief, has written the new guide, giving two reasons to justify the venture: to overcome "a lack of pin money" and to offer a "Guideline for the Masses on Popular Routes."

The introduction reflects some of the concerns and attitudes of the new generation. No climbing history whatsoever appears, yet the hours of the liquor store are given, as well as the locations of the two pubs. Climbers can stay in campgrounds, but a quieter spot might be at "a friendly waitress's apartment in Squamish." No geology is given, but we learn that granola and sprouts cannot be bought in town.

But introductions aren't the meat of any book. How are the route descriptions handled? At first glance they appear to be a bit disjointed. Carefully avoiding complete sentences or any trace of punctuation, the author lists the obligatory opening information: route name, first ascenders, difficulty, and time taken. The descriptions which follow generally *do* contain complete, readable sentences, though, once again, punctuation is conspicuous by its absence. The information is succinct and accurate. Excellent photographs, with dotted route lines, accompany the text.

Smaill is not at his best when he attempts to convey humor; his efforts often come out looking a little bit corny, not to mention highly provincial. Also, his writing style seems distinctly odd: "If you smile on tipped off blades in prying horror stories, and 40 foot lead outs free off cliffhangers on prayers, you'll be laughing when you pull on to the summit. An exceptionally fine route anywhere, the Black Dyke consists of fifteen pitches.... This climb turns into a veritable bag of liver in the rain."

Nevertheless, guidebooks don't have to be well-written to be useful. The *Squamish Chief Guide* is a well-designed book which contains a wealth of useful information for the rockclimber. **Steve Roper.**

The Climber's Guide to the High Sierra. Amateur writers have produced some very good climbing guidebooks. The task is often relatively simple: collect route descriptions for a specific area, write them up, and publish them with photos and sketches. Steve Roper is perhaps the best guidebook writer in America, a real *pro*, but the job of doing a guide to the High Sierra was almost beyond him.

Unlike seven-square-mile Yosemite Valley, where Roper produced a fine guidebook, the High Sierra consists of thousands of square miles of varied terrain, sprinkled with pockets of intense climbing activity. Many recent climbers believe that routes should not be published, and they have not cooperated with requests for information. The previous edition of the Sierra guide, published in 1972, was a poorly researched exercise in self-aggrandizement that omitted all technical climbs and left huge gaps in the Sierra record. Roper's task was indeed Herculean.

No guidebook in America has ever been so thoroughly botched as the 1972 Sierra guide, edited by Andrew J. Smatko. The book never should have been published, but since the majority of complaints with the manuscript had to do with technical climbs, a snap decision was made. The publisher merely amputated the diseased parts, leaving a grotesque torso devoid of all fifth and sixth class routes. Roper's original task was to write a separate guide to these routes, but it became apparent, immediately after publication, that the disease had not been confined to the guide's extremities. It had a cancerous growth in the form of several hundred new peaks—all, it seemed, first ascended by the guide's editor.

Roper took on the job of totally rewriting the Smatko book and adding eleven years of technical climbs. He viewed all the important areas from both the ground and the air, sometimes flying awed climbers at arm's length from their routes in his own Cessna, while craning his neck to see the details of the cliff. Jim Stuart accompanied him on several of these flights and produced a fine essay of aerial photographs for the guide.

The new book is innovative and controversial. My first impression was one of sterility. Gone are the personalized accounts of legendary climbers, listed under their peaks with terse descriptions of bivouacs or bold leads. The body of the book is cold geographical facts about routes. The names of the first ascenders are lumped into a 47-page appendix that resembles a small-town telephone directory. Tales of human interest are cubbyholed into brief chapter introductions of two to six pages. These are brilliantly and concisely written, beginning with the lay of the land, wending through Muirs or Brewers, and noting a modern climber or two before ending at the brink of the route descriptions, where Sierra ridges, chimneys and couloirs become as stark and impersonal as when first exposed to the sun by the retreating Pleistocene ice.

The book's loopholes are regrettable but wholly understandable in the face of the preceding void. Perhaps the weakest coverage is of winter ascents, which would have been better left out than handled half-heartedly. Roper states that winter ascents often have little meaning because conditions are sometimes mild, but then proceeds to record some ideal-weather climbs and neglect other far

more significant ones. Although all eleven 14,000-foot peaks have been climbed in winter, ascents of only four are mentioned. Winter technical climbs suffer equally, and ascents of the Direct North Buttress of Mt. Morrison and the East Face of Keeler Needle are missing.

The biggest cause of missing entries in the guide is the new ethic that wishes not to record climbs. Roper sympathizes with the underlying reasons and says that he has "made only a half-hearted attempt to pry this information out of climbers who feel strongly about the subject." Areas such as Tuolumne Meadows and the Palisades suffer especially, with at least a quarter of the routes—often the finest ones—not listed in the guide.

While I sympathize with the wish to protect the mountain environment by not attracting people, I no longer believe that the issue is simplistic. As a writer, I am highly suspicious of *any* movement that tries to restrict the use of language.

"The Guidebook Problem," *Ascent*, 1974, opened my eyes toward a somewhat cynical viewpoint. Admiration was expressed for a person who shares climbs with friends but doesn't write them up. Here was the hidden answer: the ethologist's rule of the flip. When search of status has nearly approached its limits in one direction, it suddenly reverses itself. Mini-skirts suddenly switched to maxis when they could go no higher. When American youth could no longer display a higher standard of living, they reversed to displaying the opposite—old clothes, simple tools, scorn of the work ethic. There was distinction and status in being as opposite to the dominant culture as possible. The same thing has happened to climbing. As possibilities for significant first ascents dwindle, it becomes fashionable not to record what used to mean status. The people who do so end up with the same exalted position among their friends that used to be accorded to those with long lists of climbs in guidebooks. Now their status comes from having "privileged" information about climbs that they share only with special friends.

Roper's new guide neatly sidesteps this behavior by completely separating the historical, factual route description from the name of the first ascent party. For the time being, the continuity of Sierra climbing history has been preserved, but if the silent flip side of recording climbs continues to play, then this may be the last edition of the guide. **Galen Rowell**

Mount McKinley Climber's Guide. What is very likely the most unique guide ever published in this country consists of a single sheet of paper, some twenty-two by thirty-five inches in size. It's the only guide I've seen which can't be called a guidebook. One side of the sheet contains a huge 1:25000 scale map of the mountain. Four routes, the Cassin Ridge, the Western Rib, the West Buttress, and the Muldrow Glacier Route, have been drawn in. The reverse side of the sheet contains clear and well-written descriptions, in both English and Japanese, of the four routes. Equipment lists, suppliers, useful addresses, and two photographs complete this side of the guide. The $5 price seems a bit high, but prospective McKinley climbers would do well to shell out the money. **Steve Roper**

The Mont Blanc Massif. This handsome guide to the classic climbing routes in the Mont Blanc region of France is a fine example of its genre—like all of Rébuffat's more recent books, it is sumptuously produced and lavishly illustrated. Although full of useful information for the alpinist who wants to visit this "homeland" of his sport, it seems almost more of a "coffee table" volume, designed as much to be savored as to be used.

But the genre itself is an interesting and somewhat contradictory one: the selected-routes guidebook, in which the author makes judgments, esthetic and practical, for the reader. A series of similar books, authored and edited in German by Walter Pause, have already become classic in the last ten years—*Im Steilen Eis, Im Steilen Fels*, the 100 most beautiful routes here, there, wherever . . . . This earlier series also includes titles such as the 100 most beautiful ski tours in the Alps, the 100 finest ski pistes, and recently a fabulous volume: *Alpen Flüssen, Kayak Flüssen*, a guide to the 50 finest whitewater kayak descents in the Alps.

The reasons why such books have been so popular and continue to be so are complex, but I suppose there is a little of the armchair mountaineer or armchair adventurer in all of us . . . . Then too, the author is substituting *his* judgment (presumably well developed and finely honed) for *ours* and this has a definite, although suspect, attrac-

117

tion for many people. Finally, none of us, however active, can climb all the great routes, or ski all the great runs, etc., in one range or on one continent . . . and while it would be nice to know a little of what one was missing, most guidebooks are intolerably dull reading, whereas these selected-routes guidebooks are really much more interesting to read.

Rébuffat's book on the Mont Blanc Range is a gem, written with a special Gallic touch that is just right for the area, and illustrated in a way that will truly make your mouth water. Something to watch for: a whole Alpine climbing vacation compressed between two covers!
Lito Tejada-Flores

Himalayan Odyssey. The reader of mountaineering literature assumes that the biography of a climber will present a series of triumphs. Beginning with the author's initial successes on the local rocks, it moves on to describe the classics of his day, details his legendary firsts, and ends with an account of the hardest way up what is then the ultimate Himalayan challenge. As a formula it works: it provides diversion for those desiring vicarious adventure and a model for those who aspire to similar success in the climbing world. Lately, however, the formula has become a bit too obvious, each replica more banal, and the conquest of each ultimate challenge more laborious. In short, we are burdened with a new genre—alpine kitsch.

Himalayan Odyssey is different. It is also quite easily one of the best books on mountaineering produced during the last decade. In one sense it is a chronicle of defeat, for Braham fails on most of the peaks he attempts; his success is of a subtler sort, one which invites reflection on the question of the authenticity of much of what now masquerades as the 'love of the mountains,' or 'love of wilderness,' or 'adventure.' Throughout the book Braham defends an attitude that is as easy to mouth as it is difficult to act upon, an attitude that values patience and familiarity to a degree quite incompatible with the vacation ethic. How many climbers can open a book with these words?

> For over thirty years, through a combination of chance and a clear affirmation of choice, I have dwelt within proximity and sometimes within sight of the great ranges of the Himalaya. Such exceptional good fortune has provided opportunities for acquiring some intimacy with these mountains, enriching yet unacquisitive, which has made them a personal and an essential part of my life.

No casual affair, this. Braham takes his mountains seriously.

Braham's familiarity with the Himalayas can only be described as astonishing. He was raised in India and, like most gentlemen there, he spent his summers in the hills. Fortunately, his parents chose Darjeeling, the famous hill station that served as the starting point for most Himalayan exploration during the 20s and 30s. Later, he attended the Jesuit college there. He thus experienced firsthand the excitement of the period, and this inspired him to begin his own journeys into the mountains. In 1949 he became an Honorary Secretary of the Himalayan Club. This position, in addition to his fluency in the local language and a knowledge of the flora and fauna of the region, provided him with an erudition that is not ordinarily found in a Himalayan climber and explains why the descriptions of his journeys are so rich in natural and historical detail. He also met all the right people. In Gangtok he meets a battered Noyce wearing one climbing boot and one "canvas" shoe. Then Tenzing passes, leading a group to the north. Later, he entertains Smythe and Tilman. And so on. Such a store of knowledge and experience could have resulted in a pompous and pedantic book, but this is not the case; instead we find a modesty and sensitivity that is no longer common in a climber.

In all some fifteen trips are described. They range from full-scale international expeditions to small, privately financed treks, scientific surveys, and solitary ascents with a Patan bodyguard. The setting for these trips is exclusively "Himalayan" in the widest sense of the term. Six of the trips are in Sikkim, two are in India, one is in Nepal, and the remainder are in Pakistan. In general, the areas are not well known, particularly when compared to such places as Khumbu or the Baltoro. Included are: the northeastern corner of Sikkim; the area around Kangchenjunga; the Gangotri region of the Garhwal; Kulu and Spiti; Minapin Peak near Rakaposhi in the Karakorum; the Siri Dara group in Swat; the Kanjiroba Himal in western Nepal; the Hindu Kush north of Chitral; the major peaks in the Kaghan valley. There are also shorter descriptions of "the limestone ranges of Quetta, sandstone mountains of lower Baluchistan, forbidden tribal hills in Waziristan, isolated escarpments in the Salt Range, and wintery Kaghan summits."

The first chapter provides a concise history of Himalayan climbing and exploration with particular emphasis on the activity during the 1920s and 1930s; the remaining chapters contain a more detailed account of exploration and climbing in the area being discussed. Each combines history and biography in a manner that is a delight to read. There is also a selection of photographs and maps. The former are rather pedestrian, but the latter are of genuine value, particularly in light of the present difficulty of obtaining maps of politically sensitive areas. Surprisingly, even the footnotes are worth reading.

While I am not in a position to question the accuracy of most of what Braham relates, I was bothered by two points. That "lone Englishman who at the turn of the century and with a handful of local men crossed a 15,000-foot ice-pass from Nagar into Ishkuman" must have gone from Naltar to Ishkuman, for there is no pass between Nagar and Ishkuman. And although official history may say that the Mir of Hunza went into exile in Chitral after his defeat by the British in 1892, I doubt it, because his great-grandson says he went to Sinkiang.

But this *is* nitpicking. It's a great book. **Jack Turner**

Mountain of Storms. Seven men died on the 1969 American Dhaulagiri Expedition. The expedition was over before the climbing even began. In 1973 the survivors of the earlier venture joined forces with new recruits for a fresh try at the same target, the "impossible" southeast ridge. This book is largely their story.

Reclining on a sunny Southwest boulder with dog and can of cold Buckhorn, it feels entirely presumptuous to review a work which is the document of so much toil and sweat, so much concern with those ultimate questions of life and death. Inevitably, the journey begins with the interminable convolutions of expedition preparation so essential to, and so removed from, mornings of glimmering untrammeled ice. Even for the reader, the expedition outfitting becomes so painfully protracted that one suspects that like many an epic climb, had the entire boggling scenario been clearly forseen it would never have been undertaken. Somehow it all gets pulled together and the group is underway to Nepal.

The book succeeds through its informality. Daring, down-covered, bearded giants discuss the horrors of cabbage and sometimes tumble into garbage pits and pig holes. That's nice to know. Exposing a few human foibles does not make an accomplishment less heroic, but imparts the kind of fragile strength that can be identified with. Mountaineering, shorn of its bravado and macho-existentialism, concerns the needs of the mass of humanity. Those things gathered in high adventure that are most worth sharing are fairly universal, common to both man the mountaineer and man the city pedestrian. They are tales of first person encounters by men in wild places, face to face with a truth that pre-exists man's most basic assumptions. The authors of *Mountain of Storms* tell their tale in an honest and unaffected manner and thus their story is a good one.

Much is divulged in a passage concerning the intensely personal and supremely female nature of the mountain. The thirst for the summit appears inseparable from the need for fulfillment that springs from deep within each of us. "Mountains, like ships or the sea, tend to be female, possibly because climbers, like sailors tend to be male," say the authors, lending more hints about the most basic incentives. The mountain begins to assume more wholistic qualities as the climber trods toward the cliffs and icefalls in his search for completeness, the yin for his yang, or the companionship of things greater than his equals. A climber locks horns with his most essential concerns, whatever they be, and is prepared to be shaken to the bone. Ron

Fear wrote in his diary of the southeast ridge ascent, "Rocks and ice were coming down around us all day—dangerous, but I love it." Harvard and Thompson supply us with more to think about than the usual expedition diet of porridge and spindrift.

There are full color plates, chronologies, and even a pictorially documented section on retinal photography, but the casual sports-fan who selects this attractive volume from the shelf where it is sandwiched by classics in golf and tennis may question whether Himalayan climbing can be considered a sport at all. Among the best passages are straight-forward descriptions of adversity that participants encountered in the form of wind and extended waits at high altitudes " . . . in the 'death zone' where gradual physical deterioration occurs regardless of diet." Fear talked about whole days when he and his tent-mate could not remember a single thing they did. The commitment to climb increases as the climber's reference to physical realities diminishes. "A man's will hardens as his body weakens, and as the distinction between dream and reality fades for a climber at high altitude, a remembered commitment is reassuringly concrete, needing no questions, no reasons, no thoughts."

The cumbersome bulk of largely unavoidable descriptions centering around the logistics reminds one of the size of the mountains involved and of the tremendous excesses of energy and equipment that expeditions periodically spill upon remote countrysides. Eventually, two men are put atop the summit via the twice-climbed northeast spur route, not the fulfillment of the dream, but still an accomplishment of no small stature. There follows the inevitable grappling with the necessity of success as imposed by the worlds outside and within. "Maybe we didn't beat the mountain, but we drank her beer for free," someone muses.

This new book points toward a new understanding of mountaineering, apparently a phenomenon peculiarly American at present. For each of us it is a personal coming of age. We seem to be growing more at peace with ourselves, and resultantly with the elements around us. Harvard and Thompson discuss the age-old tradition of the summit flag: "Once a symbol of conquest with roots in the Chauvinism of exploration, and in keeping with the man-over-nature approach to climbing a mountain, flags are now more a symbol of communion, of the spirit with which climbers and mountains become one, sharing secrets." Even faint whispers of great secrets make a journey worthwhile. A mountaineer/journalist realizes to how shallow a depth he can bring his audience through words alone. *Mountain of Storms* sheds some light on the lives that make up the big expedition and supplies a few broad hints at what they found there, but as there can be no substitute for personal experience when it comes to those things that really matter, even the best of books can only serve as a colorful road map to hallowed places where secrets may be hunted. **Jeff Salz**

Tierra del Fuego: the Fatal Lodestone. Eric Shipton's most recent book divides naturally into two parts which, unfortunately, are alike in having nothing to do with each other. The bulk of the chapters deal with the exploration, by sea, of Tierra del Fuego and the settlement of Isla Grande by the Bridges family; the first and last chapters are vignettes of the author's journeys in the region in 1962. Why the publisher has fused them into a single book is beyond me. Fortunately, the book's virtues greatly outweigh this flaw: the history is exciting, the author's trips suggestive of what remains to be done in the interior, and both are presented in that lucid prose for which Shipton is justly famous.

The tip of South America is a confusion of peaks, glaciers, and barren islands embedded in a watery labyrinth that is acknowledged to be the most dangerous in the world. It is a land notorious for its inclemency, famous for its grandeur. Less well known is the violence of its history; indeed, one is not inclined to think of it as having much of a history. There was a time, however, when it was the hub of colonial conflict between England and Spain; later, during the 19th century, it suffered the consequences of Victorian righteousness.

Shipton's description of this history is at once vivid and sad. He chronicles the famous voyages of Magellan, Drake, Sarmiento, Skyring, and Fitzroy, voyages filled with the suspense and fortitude that is the basic stuff of great adventure and punctuated with episodes of horror that are all the more chilling because they are presented so lightly. Most of the facts speak for themselves: during a twenty-five-year period in the middle of the 16th century 2,000 mariners lost their lives in these waters; of the twenty-one ships involved, only one, Magellan's ever reached Europe again via the Pacific, and it reached there without Magellan. The main problem, of course, was the weather. One especially severe storm blew Drake from the Pacific back into the Atlantic, destroyed one of his ships, permanently separated him from another, and left several of his men stranded on a bleak island. This storm lasted *fifty-two days*.

Present too were the more common sources of violence: greed, grandiosity, and stupidity played their usual roles in the drama. Mutineers were "drawn and quartered and hung on gibbets"; two of the most famous captains, Stokes and Fitzroy, committed suicide. Of the three indigenous Indian tribes, two are extinct, the victims of European disease. The remaining one—the Alakaluf—has only a hundred members.

Today Tierra del Fuego is again a place of peace and solitude, its fragile beauty intact despite (or because of?) the violence of its setting. And that explains, perhaps, why Shipton has traveled there so often.

In the spring of 1962 Shipton went on two expeditions to Tierra del Fuego. The first of these had three objectives: the ascents of Monte Darwin and Cerro Yahgan, and the crossing of the Cordillera Darwin from Brookes Bay to

NATIVES OF TIERRA DEL FUEGO.

the Beagle Channel. Together with three Chilean companions, Shipton succeeded in achieving all these goals. The second trip, an attempt to reach Monte Burney on the Munos Gamero Peninsula, was unsuccessful due to a shortage of time. In both cases the expeditions used what are now the classic methods for travel in the region. An inflatable rubber boat with a motor is used for the approach, a path is found (or forced) through the thick forests surrounding the fiords, and the usual alpine procedures are used to reach the goal.

Time has not changed the weather. Mists and fogs and severe winds abound; the peaks still appear unexpectedly close only to disappear again for days, or weeks, or months. There is a certain seriousness about this wilderness. Things are always a bit desperate, and it is unlikely that it will be forced to endure the multi-colored minions of our wilderness societies. Even Shipton is moved to remark that "For all its haunting beauty, there was an atmosphere of hostility about this land, as though it resented our intrusion."

Shipton's descriptions of these trips are rather sketchy. His companions remain ghostly characters and the climbs are almost incidental to the narrative. Indeed, the ascents of Monte Darwin and Cerro Yahgan receive only a paragraph each, hardly enough to qualify it as a book on mountaineering. It is instead a book on exploration, and as such it achieves something quite rare: a sense of the land and its atmosphere that suggests the source of its strange attraction. Jack Turner.

Downward Bound—A Mad Guide to Rock Climbing.
Downward Bound is a major literary event in the life of reading-minded people who might have any interest in mountains, mountaineers and adventure, or even in an adventurous man such as "Beasto" Harding who climbs, drinks, and feels, and somehow has enough energy left over to put it all into poignant, believable, crazy words of the English tongue. Harding, whom I have never climbed with and barely know personally, (but would and do respect, like, love, and will always listen to) has the ability to encapsulate and summarize the key issue: What in hell is climbing all about anyway? I first encountered the grizzled old devil in Truckee, on his way to Yosemite to do "a little climbing." I mean, anyone who lives in Truckee can't be all bad, no matter what deranged "zones" he has encountered; no matter that he shares the hard, fun, unaccepted (socially) truth that "in wine there is truth" (lots of folks, climbers included, don't like dealing with truth). Besides, Harding is the only major climber in America who has taken a stand consistent enought to trust ... I had that knowledge in my gut before I read his book.

The first sixty-four pages, however, are so boring and unreadable as to almost break the book, and I know people who have given up the chase before proceeding further. I don't blame them, but they made a huge mistake. On page 65, Warren starts to get into what it is that he wants to or has to say (he was paid an advance to write the book). And what he has to say is wonderful. It is also subtle, informational, pertinent, and as sharp as personality/character analysis-assassination-assuming gets in terms of climbers as real people.

For Harding, climbing, in essence, involves a love for the mountains and a desire to have fun, nothing more. This is simple, easy to understand, and somehow more straightforward and reliable than the grossly complex "ethical" homilies laid down by some of Harding's critics who, interestingly enough, often have a hard time aligning their practices with their preachings. Harding also avoids the heaviness of telling other climbers what they should or should not think.

Warren Harding/*Photo Galen Rowell*

As a matter of fact, Harding's un-heavy, matter-of-fact, straightforward, light, funny perspective on climbing, climbers (himself included), the climbing world/scene is the very thing that makes *Downward Bound* a major event. It is one of the few climbing books that is as much fun to read as a good route is to climb, and the attentive, interested reader has a fair chance to learn something. It is carried out with the technique of presenting a manuscript of a taped slide show presentation; a question and answer between Batso, giving the show, and various recognizable stereotypes in the audience. For instance:

"YOUNG NOVICE CLIMBER: . . . I get so much feedback about what a serious business this climbing is. Not just because it's risky, but from a moralistic standpoint. Like I came to camp 4 in Yosemite for the first time last summer to expand my limited climbing experience. But I was treated like an outsider. No one was very friendly or helpful, and I felt put down—for not having the "proper attitude," I suppose. Is it really all so heavy?

"BATSO: No. But some people have a longing for structured, institutionalized conduct. They also tend to view themselves as responsible for the morality of climbers. For them, climbing becomes an ideology, a religion. They often attempt to convert all climbers to their tenets. This frequently takes the form of strongly worded articles appearing in climbing journals and guides.

"Others are more relaxed; they conduct their climbing in a manner pleasing and meaningful to them personally. They are not impressed with the self-ordained leaders of the climbing community and their edicts.

"This pretty well describes my own personal climbing philosophy. I simply like to be in the mountains and *climb*, without worrying about a bunch of bullshit. As we move along, we'll see that this has been the basis for quite a bit of spirited discussion. I'm considered an anarchist by many in the climbing hierarchy, but there seem to be many who feel that a little anarchy, in a world edging ever closer to 1984, may very well be a good thing."

In my opinion, it is not only "a good thing," it is like a drink of cold mountain stream water on a hot day with a heavy pack. One aspect of the book that appealed to me (though it offended Tom Higgins in *Mountain 44*) is that Harding, who, as a climber of long standing and impeccable merit has obviously dealt many times *personally* with the possibility of death, can laugh about death without tarnishing his clear respect for the climbers who have met it. In the appendix he has a very subtle and accurate "Glossary of Climbers According to the Zone System" which contains descriptions of Bill Feuerer, who committed suicide, and Jim Madsen, who rappelled off the end of his rope near the top of El Capitan.

"DOLT (WILLIAM FEUERER)   IMPOSSIBLE TO RATE
"This wonderfully insane, wildly creative fellow is simply beyond any zone rating. Dolt lent speed, dash, and general insecurity to many early climbing epics. He turned out to be a little crazier than we thought. For reasons best known to himself, Dolt saw fit to move on to the Big Wall in the Sky a few years back.

"JIM MADSEN   ZONE 2 (HONORARY ZONE 1)
"This curious dual rating is appropriate in this case. In spite of his fantastic climbing prowess, J.M. lacked the necessary evangelical zeal to qualify for zone 1; hence the zone 2 rating. However, in recognition of his incredible speed-record-setting descent of the face of El Capitan (this record was recently equaled but not surpassed), *Downward Bound* feels compelled to bestow an honorary zone 1 rating posthumously." Though Higgins writes that all this "simply is not funny," I think it is both funny and refreshing.

Much of the book concerns the controversial first two ascents of The Wall of the Early Morning Light, both of which are well documented in other places. The version in *Downward Bound* is the best I've read. In it, as through the entire book, Harding reveals himself as a warm, sensitive, intelligent though admittedly wine-soaked, humorous, tough *human*, who one instinctively likes. His lack of venom and vindictiveness toward his critics and their venemous, vindictive tirades against him is revealing of the man.

The photos are good but poorly reproduced, but the cartoons by Beryl "Beasto" Knauth are really funny. It is a book I recommend to climbers and non-climbers alike, but, then, I have weaknesses for anarchy, honesty, climbing, wine, humor, irreverence, and for a good story, which *Downward Bound* is. **Dick Dorworth**

Climbing in North America. Chris Jones has pulled off a rare feat among climbing histories. His treatment of the topic is truly exhaustive, yet he definitely avoids becoming exhausting. His welter of names, routes, ranges, and events could easily have blurred into just another extended laundry list, but his flair for characterization and intimate anecdote rescues his research from becoming overpowering. I found myself looking forward eagerly to the next vignette. What can Jones come up with to equal the glorious quote from Jean Weber's *Journal* detailing the first ascent of Mt. Alberta? The answer: the detailed contents of Norman Clyde's pack. And what to equal the tale of Ad Carter's recovery of the lost plans for the Normandy invasion? Obviously the description of Salathé hauling his second up the Bathtub Pitch on the Higher Cathedral Spire in a state of extreme undress. Not all his cameos come off so well, but there are ample samples to fit a wide variety of tastes, and on the whole they exhibit a rare standard of liveliness.

Despite the excellence of its detail, however, it is in its total sweep that Jones' story delivers its greatest impact. The interweaving of the climbing traditions from the various geographical centers is masterfully done. He exhibits clearly the long period of isolation in which developments in style and technique occurred as regional specialties with virtually no cross-fertilization. I remember well the disdain with which the Teton regulars of the early 1950s looked upon the occasional "Gunker" who dared to venture onto their turf. Stories were told and retold of their inept routefinding, forced bivouacs on Symmetry, etc., etc. In the light of Jones' narrative it becomes apparent that the Shawangunk climbers of that day were so superior in pure rockclimbing ability that the Teton buff simply *had* to put them down in terms of big mountain know-how. It was the only competitive edge they had.

The way in which such regionalism has gradually given way to a genuine "American Climbing Style" seems to me to be the major message of the book. The clear depiction of the interplay between the Northeast, Colorado, Tetons, Yosemite, and the Northwest as techniques and standards slowly develop and coalesce makes a fascinating thread upon which to string the yarns and characters. I suspect that all climbers reading this volume will have in mind favorite stories which they wish Jones had included. (Mine is of Glenn Exum, wearing football shoes, balking three times at the corner of Wall Street—on his solo first ascent of the Exum Ridge on the Grand Teton—before finally jumping the gap.) But the test of quality is surely the instant urge to re-read sections of the book as soon as one has finished it—in order to fix in mind certain new stories which were here encountered for the first time.

My own only real regret at the close of the book was that Jones had devoted himself so utterly to the history of the growth of standards and techniques that he short-changed the feeling tone and broader motivations which have long characterized the climbing game. The few hints he has given us only whet the appetite for a more lengthy treatment of these generally neglected aspects of the sport. Perhaps another volume could be coaxed from Jones' pen with this in mind. It is almost worth wishing another skiing accident upon him to ensure such a happy outcome. **Willi Unsoeld**

Beginner's Guide to Rock and Mountain Climbing. Most climbing manuals are either unreadable or have missing and incorrect information. Some have both. Exceptions are Royal Robbins' *Rockcraft* series and the Seattle Mountaineers' *Mountaineering: The Freedom of the Hills*, and, now, the Mendenhalls' *Beginner's Guide to Rock and Mountain Climbing*.

Where Robbins' books cover only rockclimbing—although in great depth— and *Freedom of the Hills* covers—at great length—all aspects of mountaineering, *Beginner's Guide* fills the gap for those who, without any previous mountaineering experience, want to learn to climb, and also those who simply want to better understand what it is that climbers do. The book is short, inexpensive, and has humorous asides. There is no attempt to describe advanced rock, ice, or general mountaineering techniques. It is written toward learning the skills necessary for easy and moderate peak climbing. (And, to that end, has a useful finish: road directions to the bases, and route descriptions to the summits, of the high Mexican volcanos.) Much of the information given might seem over-obvious to anyone familiar with climbing skills, but I think that most climbers, and most climbing instructors, forget how confusing their world was when they entered it, and how awed they were by it. The Mendenhalls, apparently, remember.

The book has its flaws: there is a confusing item on the testing of pitons. It is suggested that after downward hammer blows, the pin can be tested further by jerking on the rope. Perhaps that should read . . . falling on the rope! Some of the illustrations are unclear, there is no explanation as to why bad piton placements are bad, and, in a cartoon depicting a leaderfall, the rope looks like it could easily lift the belayer's legs and come out from around him. Perhaps the greatest criticism that could be levied is that the Mendenhalls seem unaware of how quickly beginners are becoming experts nowadays.

The book excludes information that a beginner will want and need to know if he is to become a competent leader, but that information is well presented elsewhere. *Beginner's Guide* fulfills its title very well. **Roger Breedlove**

Hard Rock: Great British Rock-Climbs. Ken Wilson, the effervescent editor of *Mountain*, has master-minded a compelling book. He selected fifty-seven famous British

rock climbs and invited a number of first-class climbers to write essays about them. Then, "to enrich the brew further," he collected pictures that complemented the text. The resulting book is not another guide to selected climbs, but an exposé of high-standard British climbing. Like its predecessor, Cleare and Smythe's 1966 *Rock Climbers in Action in Snowdonia, Hard Rock* is about climbers and their *raison d'être*.

The book's most engaging characteristic is the enthusiasm that runs through its pages. Although differing in their style and approach, the books varied authors are confirmed rock addicts. We see them gripped up on the crag and relaxed in the bar; furtive about their plans yet generous to their rivals; playing the game for laughs and playing it for keeps. The perennial question "why do people climb," is answered by the joy and exhilaration revealed by the authors.

As I dipped into the book the images came alive. Glencoe on a chill autumn day; thundering surf below an Angelsey sea cliff; Robin Smith on the crags of Ben Nevis. I lived again the author's fears as they faced the crux, their frustration as they tried to arrange protection, and their relief when the worst was over. I asked myself what I was doing sitting in a chair; why wasn't I up in the mountains this very moment? A book that moves us this strongly must be written from the heart.

The book's shortcomings are solely the literary failure of a few individual authors. They were unable to evoke their chosen climbs, and their accounts are little more than dressed-up guidebook descriptions. However, the bulk of the essays are sufficiently vivid that we pass over the pedestrian accounts. For anyone who wonders about the why of climbing and for all rock addicts, this book is a must. **Chris Jones**

Encyclopaedia of Mountaineering. It is no easy task to read an entire encyclopedia; it certainly doesn't qualify as pleasure reading. When it rests alongside other books at the bedside, it is the last to be chosen. Yet, over the course of several evenings I managed to thread my way from Abalakov, the father of Russian climbing, to Zurcher, a Swiss mountaineer. A sample page includes the following entries: Corrie, Corsica, Cottian Alps, Couloir, Courmayeur, John Jermyn Cowell, Cow's Tail, Anthony D.M. Cox, Crack, and Crag Lough. Names, places, techniques, history; all are covered. But covered how well?

The most obvious criticism of the encyclopedia is its incredible bias. Of the 450-odd names of famous or noteworthy climbers which appear under the main listings, two-thirds are British. Here are just a few names which do *not* merit our attention: Contamine, Couzy, Frendo, Harlin, Hiebeler, Herrligkoffer, Herzog, Lachenal, Lambert, Muir, Roch, Ullman, and Whitaker. Included, however, are scores of entries such as: "Donald Duff—inventor of the Duff Stretcher for mountain rescue and first chairman of the Mountain Rescue Committee for Scotland." Or how about Walter Leaf: "A London banker who made a number of minor new routes and first ascents in the Alps between 1871 and 1893. His brother Herbert Leaf was with him for the first two seasons."

The British coverage seems remarkably complete and informative and in Britain I would think the book will be well received. After all, many important climbers in history, especially the early years of alpinism, came from the Commonwealth.

Let me mention a few things I learned from this book about mountaineering. Barry Bishop became "the first American to reach the summit of Mount Everest." The technique rockclimbers refer to as a mantelshelf is called "chinning" by the Americans. Harrer climbed the Eigerwand in 1935. Shiprock, in New Mexico, is "a group of spires." Overhangs "are climbed by artificial means." The only effective treatment for frostbite is "to increase the supply of oxygen." Colorado mountains are all referred to as "14ers." Cecil Slingsby died in 1924 and again, "peacefully at his home," in 1929.

I learned a great deal about 100-foot-high outcrops in England but nothing about Cerro Fitzroy except its first ascent date. I learned that King Albert of Belgium died rappelling, yet all biographies I have read indicate that he somehow pulled off a large block while on a summit and took the dreaded groundfall. I learned that the confusing Diamir region of Nanga Parbat is truly confusing; never using this spelling, the author gives us three more: Diamiri, Diamiari, and Diamirai (the latter is actually correct for a pass).

Many of these inaccuracies, or half-inaccuracies, are relatively unimportant. In the more than a thousand entries I found, in six hours, only about fifty errors or so, and many of these were simple typos which should have been caught. Basically, there is a vast amount of information about British climbing history. But don't depend on this work for the truth—check other sources. **Steve Roper.**

Mountains. John Cleare's new book is a disappointment.

In 1966 when I first saw *Rock Climbers in Action in Snowdonia*—illustrated by Cleare—I was much impressed, and even now it is my opinion that it is the best published collection of rockclimbing photographs. In 1973 Cleare, with Robin Collomb, published *Sea Cliff Climbing in Britain*. The photographs illustrating that book did not have the same qualities that I had so much admired. When *Mountains* was published I hoped that it would be closer in quality to the Snowdonia book. It is not. Unlike the other books, Cleare is the sole author of this new book and supplies most of the photographs and text, although credit is given to Chris Baxter for the information on Australia, New Zealand, and New Guinea.

I have much to malign in *Mountains*, too much in fact, for this short review. Some of the low points: The design of the book—probably its strongest point—has, in my opinion, one serious flaw. Many of the photographs are printed across the crease between facing pages, a feature that can ruin the effect of even the best photographs.

Cleare is known for his photography, but his abilities could not be shown by way of the reproductions in this book. Many of the photographs, including the twenty-two credited to others, look washed out and have little detail. Some of the captions call attention to peaks in the background that are barely discernible gray humps in the sky. Some plates are printed out of register, causing them to look like cardboard paste-ups. I compared the three books Cleare has illustrated: the reproduction, although best in the Snowdonia book, was nearly the same. The photographs themselves seem to drop in quality. There are good photographs in *Mountains*, but there are many poor and mediocre ones.

The text includes geographies and climbing histories and is divided into seven chapters: The European Alps, North America; Britain; Africa; Himalaya; Australia, New Zealand and New Guinea; "And the Rest." In the areas with which Cleare is most familiar there are personal accounts of ascents and a few tales. The geographies and histories work the best, but there is nothing there that

could not be better read elsewhere, except, perhaps, the section on Australia and New Zealand.

Cleare's prose, except for the lyrical introduction, is indifferent. The personal accounts of ascents includes an over-long, forgettable description of a love affair with a mountain in the Alps, a story of how and why he failed to get up a 5.7 slab route in Yosemite (piton-damaged cracks won't take nuts), and how he and Tom Patey climbed a British sea stack, an account which dies of too much "out right onto the wall of an overhanging beak, across, up, and a mantelshelf," ad nauseam. I would think that with so many books out about climbing, an author would know how seldom route descriptions work as literature. If the opposite were true, guidebooks would be on the best-seller lists.

Of the portraits of outstanding mountaineers that the book jacket promises, Patey, who is best remembered for his wit and ordinary humanness, sounds and acts just like all other hard men, saying hard-man lines as he slips off into the mist to do hard-man deeds, as the mortals gape in idolization. Cleare's biographical sketch of Royal Robbins, while an informed view, left me with a fuzzy-edged, sentimental picture of Robbins and his family standing under the sign of their Modesto mountain shop.

Cleare apparently holds the antiquated idea that mountaineering is a wellspring in the British isles that flows outward to the rest of the world in diminishing circles. *Mountains* looks like it will offer a picture of world mountaineering, and the table of contents supports that view. But nearly one half of the book deals with climbing in Britain and the Alps. That, in itself, is fair enough, but Cleare's entire reference to South America is only three pages long. Cleare states it is necessary to make his book complete, but I wonder what his idea of complete is. North American geographies and histories are covered in one and one half pages. Cleare does tell us, however, that in their vast expanse of mountains, Americans are lucky.

Near the end of the book Cleare gives an apologetic

paragraph for only just touching on the mountains in each continent, but I'm sure that he hopes you buy his book before you find out that it is a low-quality hodgepodge. *Mountains* cannot be called a history, an overview, an autobiography, or an interesting book. **Roger Breedlove.**

Big Wall Climbing. Doug Scott's *Big Wall Climbing* is an ambitious book. It is no less than a worldwide history of big wall climbing, a treatise on its methods, and a where-to guide for big wall aspirants. Scott is no stranger to ambitious projects; his own climbing has encompassed innovative big wall routes in Asia and Baffin Island, as well as several expeditions to the southwest face of Mount Everest. He is therefore able to bring to his work a singular advantage: he sees the action through the eyes of an insider. The disadvantage of having an insider's viewpoint, of course, is that his outlook may be colored by personal bias. Scott seems happily free of prejudice (or perhaps the reviewer shares his prejudice). Indeed, his viewpoint is more objective than that of several other mountain historians, most of whom were not first-class mountaineers.

The major part of the book is devoted to history; the last two sections on method and big wall climbing areas account for just a third of the text. The latter sections are well done, but one cannot help wondering who will use them. Certainly people learn to climb from books, but once they are considering a trip to Patagonia it seems they would be getting their knowledge from companions rather than instruction books. The real meat, and value of, Scott's work is the section on the development of big wall climbing. What, however, does he mean by big wall? In the introduction he refers to expected areas such as the Dolomites and Yosemite, but in the next paragraph goes on to include practically every mountain range in the world. The problem Scott faced is that it is difficult to tell where big wall climbing ends and where rockclimbing or alpinism begins. Furthermore, it may not be helpful to do so; a discussion of big wall climbing divorced from its natural extensions would be a bastard entity. What Scott gives us is a condensed history of climbing in the Alps, although he is unsure just what to allow under his "big wall" umbrella. He talks about several predominantly ice climbs (Eigerwand, Les Droites), but later feels he should limit his discussion, prefacing a paragraph with "Although the Matterhorn North Face is not a rock wall, it would be incomplete . . . ." In spite of his ambiguity over the subject matter his history does hang together.

The best parts of the history are where Scott discusses a subject at length or puts forward a point of view. Here his writing is fair to the individuals concerned, yet persuasively argues the case for a pure climbing style. However, the gut information in the history, the people and places, the when and the why, are not always so deftly handled. Several chapters are readily understood, but others tend to blur in front of the mind. There is such a profusion of names, dates, and grades, that individual people and events are virtually indistinguishable. Scott has chosen to put the maximum amount of data into the book, rather than bring out key individuals and events. This reviewer wished that Scott had dwelt on less information at greater length, but then others would probably object that he had left out important facts!

What of the history itself? The sections on the Alps and Britain are accurate and well balanced. Scott had a wealth of source material to draw upon and did so to good effect. If his treatment of North America is less successful, we must acknowledge that there is no worthwhile history to which he could turn. He had the difficult task of researching from several thousand miles distance (although his visits to Yosemite paid handsome dividends on that particular section). Scott's worst gaffe about North America is his statement about Wiessner's 1937 ascent of Devil's Tower: "It was twenty years before American climbers were establishing routes of comparable difficulty." By Wiessner's own estimate the north ridge of the Grand Teton (Underhill/Fryxell 1931) was more difficult than Devil's Tower. The omission of any explanation of the American rating system is unfortunate; it is confusing to read of Grade VI climbs of the 1920s in the Eastern Alps and later to be told that the 1957 ascent of the northwest face of Half Dome was the first Grade VI in North America. A European Grade VI and an American Grade VI may not be remotely comparable; the first is a measure of technical difficulty, akin to our 5th class decimal ratings, the latter an assessment of overall difficulty. The last part of the history is a discussion of big wall climbing in remote areas. The selections here are hard to understand. There is a half page on the High Sierra but three lines on the Alaska Range; fourteen pages on Patagonia but not a mention of the rest of the Andean chain.

Scott has written an important book that has something worthwhile to say to everyone interested in the big walls. Its shortcomings are far outweighed by its strengths, and the greatest strengths are Scott's thoughtful analyses. **Chris Jones.**

This book is set in 10-point Theme—the IBM version of Optima, designed by the celebrated Swiss typographer Hermann Zapt—and printed on 80-pound Cameo Dull. The illustrations are reproduced in 300-line duotone. Composition and printing by Pacific Rotaprinting Company, Berkeley, California. Designed by Lito Tejada-Flores.